Ready for PET

Teacher's Book

Nick Kenny   Anne Kelly

Macmillan Education
4 Crinan Street, London N1 9XW
A division of Macmillan Publishers Limited
Companies and representatives throughout the world

ISBN 978-0-230-02074-0

Text © Nick Kenny and Anne Kelly
Design and illustration © Macmillan Publishers Limited 2007

First published 2001
This edition 2007

All rights reserved; no part of this publication may be reproduced, stored in a retrieval system, transmitted in any form, or by any means, electronic, mechanical, photocopying, recording, or otherwise, without the prior written permission of the publishers.

Original design by Inperspective
This edition by Carolyn Gibson
Cover design by Andrew Oliver

The authors would like to thank Barbara Lewis, David Foll, Penny Beck, Margaret van Doelen, Nelson Aurich, Graciela Mazzucco and Russell Crew-Gee for their help with this book.

Printed in Thailand
2017 2016 2015 2014
13 12 11 10 9 8 7

Contents

Introduction
	What is the Preliminary English Test (PET)?	2
	The format of the PET examination	3
	What a PET student needs to know	4
	How the teacher can help	4
	Standards and assessment	5
	Assessment of writing	5
	Assessment of speaking	6
	How to use *Ready for PET*	7

Teaching notes
Unit 1	Lesson 1: Personal information	8
	Lesson 2: A regular thing	10
Unit 2	Lesson 1: You live and learn	12
	Lesson 2: All the best books	14
Unit 3	Lesson 1: Holiday adventures	16
	Lesson 2: Just the job	18
Unit 4	Lesson 1: House and home	20
	Lesson 2: Interesting people	22
Unit 5	Lesson 1: Places of interest	24
	Lesson 2: Getting there	27
Unit 6	Lesson 1: What a bargain!	28
	Lesson 2: City life	31
Unit 7	Lesson 1: Food and drink	32
	Lesson 2: Your own space	35
Unit 8	Lesson 1: Close to nature	37
	Lesson 2: The wide world	39
Unit 9	Lesson 1: Free time	41
	Lesson 2: Get well soon!	42
Unit 10	Lesson 1: Entertainment	44
	Lesson 2: The age of communication	46

Key to Practice Test 1	48
Key to Practice Test 2	49
Recording Script for Practice Test 1	50
Notes on the sample Speaking test	53
Recording Script for Practice Test 2	54
Examples of student writing	57
Wordlist	61

Introduction

Ready for PET is for lower-intermediate students of English who are preparing for the University of Cambridge Preliminary English Test (PET). It consists of a Coursebook, a Teacher's Book, and an Audio CD plus a CD-ROM with six PET practice tests.

The Coursebook deals with language and skills development, and is available in two editions. (The 'with key' edition of the Coursebook includes a key to exercises and Recording Scripts; the other edition does not have these.)

The Teacher's Book explains the content of PET and gives advice about preparing students for it. It also includes detailed notes on the lessons. Answer keys and Recording Scripts are an integral part of the Teacher's Book. The accompanying Audio CD has recordings of all the listening exercises.

Ready for PET can be used in a variety of situations. It can be used in class as an integrated part of a programme of study. Or, if only a few students in the class are planning to take PET, it can be used by the teacher to give extra homework or private study assignments to these students. Students can, of course, use *Ready for PET* by themselves to prepare for the test without the help of a teacher. For more advice on how to use *Ready for PET,* see page 7.

If they have a test as their goal, students have a greater motivation to study. The language skills needed to complete the test tasks in PET are needed in the real world, and language qualifications are becoming more and more important in higher education and in the workplace. Students who succeed at PET gain confidence in their skills and acquire test experience. This will help them to go on to do well in higher-level examinations.

What is the Preliminary English Test (PET)?

PET is an examination in general English at University of Cambridge ESOL Level 2. It forms part of the five-level main suite of examinations offered by Cambridge. The level of the PET examination corresponds to Level 2 in the Association of Language Testers in Europe (ALTE) scale, and to the Council of Europe's Threshold level. As it forms part of a wider system of language levels, PET enjoys a high degree of recognition among educators and employers worldwide.

The following table shows how ALTE, Cambridge and Council of Europe language levels correspond to one another:

ALTE LEVEL	CAMBRIDGE ESOL EXAM	COUNCIL OF EUROPE LEVEL
1	Key English Test (KET)	Waystage A2
2	Preliminary English Test (PET)	Threshold B1
3	First Certificate in English (FCE)	B2
4	Certificate in Advanced English (CAE)	C1
5	Certificate of Proficiency in English (CPE)	C2

PET is widely taken by students who are hoping to go on and take the higher level Cambridge examinations such as the First Certificate in English (FCE), Certificate in Advanced English (CAE) and the Certificate of Proficiency in English (CPE). For these students, PET represents an important stepping stone as they develop their language skills. For other students, especially those who will only use English occasionally in a professional context, PET represents a final learning goal.

The PET examination is taken in countries all over the world, by people of all ages. It has proved particularly suitable for teenagers and young adults in secondary and tertiary education.

PET aims to test students' practical use of English in the real world. At this level, students should have the language skills necessary to deal with everyday situations which call for a largely predictable use of language. PET focuses on reading, writing, speaking and listening, and tests both receptive and productive language skills.

In terms of receptive skills, students are expected to deal with texts found in everyday life. For example, they should be able to retrieve information relevant to their everyday needs from signs, notices, packaging, guidebooks, brochures, etc. In addition, they should be able to read and understand the main points in informal notes, letters, magazine articles, and other everyday texts.

Similarly, students are expected to be able to retrieve information from spoken texts such as public announcements, guided tours, sets of instructions, and informational broadcasts, such as weather forecasts. They should also be able to understand the gist of simple informal conversations.

Introduction

In terms of productive skills, students are expected to be able to ask for general information in everyday situations. They should have the linguistic skills to ask for further information, or for clarification if necessary. In a work or study context, students should be able to take part in a discussion where factual information or simple opinions and attitudes are exchanged. They are not, however, expected to deal with the unpredictable or unfamiliar. Students should therefore be able to take and pass on simple telephone messages, as long as the information is of a routine nature. Similarly, students should be able to write simple personal letters or short narratives, especially where these conform to a fairly standard format.

The format of the PET examination

There are four main components in PET, tested in three papers. Each of the four components (Reading, Writing, Listening and Speaking) carries 25% of the final mark. Two of the components, Reading and Writing, are assessed in a combined paper. Each of the papers is divided into a number of separate parts, representing different tasks that the candidates have to complete.

The three papers are organized as follows:

Paper 1: Reading and Writing (1 hour 30 minutes)

Part	Skill	Text type	Task type	Test focus
1	Reading	signs, messages	multiple-choice	detailed understanding
2	Reading	short texts	matching	skimming and scanning
3	Reading	factual text	true/false	scan for information
4	Reading	text with attitude/opinion	multiple-choice	global understanding
5	Reading	factual text	multiple-choice cloze	knowledge of grammar and vocabulary
1	Writing	sentences	trans-formations	grammatical accuracy
2	Writing	short message	giving information	linguistic competence
3	Writing	informal letter or story	writing letter or narrative	linguistic competence

Paper 2: Listening (30 minutes)

Part	Text type	Task type	Test focus
1	short texts	multiple-choice	gist meaning
2	factual monologue/dialogue	multiple-choice	understanding detail
3	factual monologue	note completion	understanding and recording detail
4	informal dialogue	true/false	attitude/opinion

Paper 3: Speaking (10–12 minutes)

Part	Input	Task type	Test focus
1	spoken rubric	conversation	giving personal information
2	visual prompt	situational dialogue	exchanging ideas and opinions
3	photograph	individual long turn	descriptive language
4	spoken rubric	freer discussion	expressing attitudes and opinions

PET candidates are awarded one overall grade for the test as a whole. The overall grade is reached by adding together the scores in each of the three papers. There are four possible overall grades:

    Pass with merit   Pass   Narrow fail   Fail

To reach a pass grade, a candidate must achieve a score of 70% or above in the test as a whole.

The PET examination is offered on six dates in the year, although only some of these will be available in most places. A computer-based version of the PET Reading, Writing and Listening tests is also offered on certain dates throughout the year. Cambridge produces written information about the examination in the *PET Handbook*, plus past paper packs and sample speaking tests on video. For further information about how to enter for the examination, or how to become an examination centre, contact:

    Cambridge ESOL
    1 Hills Road
    Cambridge
    CB1 2EU
    United Kingdom
    Tel: (0)1223 553074
    www.cambridgeESOL.org

What a PET student needs to know

Most good, lower-intermediate, general English coursebooks which develop the four skills of reading, writing, listening and speaking equally contain all the language a student needs to know for PET. *Ready for PET* builds on this basic knowledge to prepare students specifically for the test.

First of all, students taking the test must be able to perform a range of common language functions in English. These include introducing themselves and other people; asking for and giving information about routines and habits; talking about past events and recent activities; talking about future or imaginary situations; expressing opinions and making choices; and so on. A full list of these language functions is given in the *PET Handbook*, published by Cambridge ESOL. *Ready for PET* focuses on all the functions that students need to do well in the test.

Secondly, students need control of the grammatical forms and patterns necessary to express these functions, such as regular and irregular verb forms, including imperatives, infinitives, gerunds and passive forms; modal verbs; simple, continuous and perfect tenses; simple reported speech; and simple clause patterns, including conditionals, time, relative and purpose clauses, and clauses with 'because' and 'although'. A full list is given in the *PET Handbook*. The Coursebook gives practice in the main grammatical areas involved.

Thirdly, students need to be able to understand and use a range of everyday vocabulary to talk about various common topics and situations. They should also be able to talk about themselves and their interests, eg nationality, subjects of study, work, hobbies, likes and dislikes. The Coursebook deals with the main topic areas.

Fourthly, students need to have developed the four language skills equally. They need to be able to understand a variety of reading and listening texts. They should also be able to express their ideas on a range of common topics fluently and coherently, in both speech and writing. In addition, they must develop strategies to help themselves when they get into difficulties, such as guessing the meanings of unknown words, asking for clarification, and paraphrasing. The Coursebook develops all four skills. The Teacher's Book places special emphasis on fluency in writing and speaking, which is necessary to do well in PET.

Finally, students need information about what the test contains, and practice doing the different types of test exercises. *Ready for PET* provides extensive and comprehensive help with these areas, including two full practice tests at the end of the Coursebook and six Reading, Writing and Listening tests on a CD-ROM.

How the teacher can help

The teacher needs to be informed about the content of the examination and the testing focus of each task. This will enable him or her to pass on reliable information about the exam, and ensure that students practise in a meaningful way.

It is assumed that students following a PET preparation course have already taken, or are taking, a general English course at the same level. In many cases PET preparation classes will be additional to the main course. For this reason *Ready for PET* does not present particular language structures.

PET preparation classes will increase students' confidence by providing practice in speaking skills and vocabulary development. Such opportunities may not normally be available in the classroom, due to the constraints of time and curriculum.

Although PET preparation classes can deal with remedial grammar work, this should not be allowed to dominate. Students need to practise examination tasks so that they gain a greater understanding of what is required and what, therefore, represents good performance.

Teachers may want to give their students a mock test at some stage during the course. The tasks in the Coursebook develop skills needed for the test and they generally have a similar format to the ones in the test. For this reason a mock test is best given at the end of the course. However, students can be encouraged to practise doing exam tasks using the CD-ROM in their own time at regular intervals throughout their exam preparation course.

A mock examination using one of the practice tests will require quite a lot of time and organization. Examination conditions should be reproduced as far as possible. To give students a true indication of what they have to do on the day, exact timings should be given. The room should be laid out so that students cannot easily speak to each other, or copy one another's work.

There are copies of Cambridge ESOL answer sheets on pages 88–89 of the Coursebook. Make sure that students know how and when these are used. In the Listening paper, they will need to write on the question paper and then copy out their answers, whereas in the Reading and Writing paper they should remember to write their answers directly onto the answer sheet.

It may be necessary to hold a mock test outside class time, or to test different papers in several lessons. Remember that students are not allowed to use dictionaries or other books during the examination, and must not be given any help by the teacher.

The Speaking test is difficult to organize in class time, and it may well prove impossible for each student in the class to have a complete mock test. If you leave it out, remember that it represents 25% of the overall result and students generally do quite well in it.

Make sure that you always give feedback on students' speaking skills, even if this is based on your general impression rather than a formal test. Usually you can err on the side of generosity with this mark, because confidence is extremely important in the Speaking paper. Students should always be praised for making an attempt at a speaking task, and teachers should avoid giving negative feedback, as this may discourage fluency.

Standards and assessment

In PET, the marks a student gains in all three papers are added together and one overall grade is given as a result of this. Each component (Reading, Writing, Listening and Speaking) carries a possible 25% of the total marks. A student does not necessarily have to 'pass' each component in order to gain an overall pass in PET. A 'pass' corresponds to 70% or more of the total overall marks.

Each question on the Reading and Listening papers, and on Part 1 of the Writing paper, is worth one mark. There are 35 marks on the Reading paper but these are adjusted so that they represent 25% of the total available marks for the whole test. Most of these questions can be objectively marked (they are either right or wrong), and students record their answers by marking an answer sheet (see pages 88–89 of the Coursebook) which can then be checked by a computer. Some of these questions (Listening Part 3 and Writing Part 1) involve writing words on the answer sheets. There may be more than one acceptable answer for each question, and so these are checked by an examiner. There is still only one mark for each question.

It is relatively easy for a teacher to see whether students are approaching the required standard for the reading and writing parts of PET. The question to ask is: 'By the end of the preparation course, are students generally getting about 70% of the practice exercises correct?'

Assessing students' performance in writing (PET Writing Parts 2 and 3) and in the Speaking paper is more complicated. Here the emphasis is on assessing positive aspects of the student's performance. The examiner will want to see how clearly and coherently the student manages to communicate ideas, rather than how many mistakes are made. The teacher should take this approach when assessing students' classwork.

Assessment of writing

There are 5 marks available for PET Writing Part 2, and 15 marks for Part 3.

In PET Writing Part 2, the student has to write a short communicative message. The focus of the assessment in this part is on how successfully the student has managed to communicate the required message. In the instrucitons the student is given three points to include. Failure to include one of these points in an answer will mean the student can score no more than three out of the five available marks. Students are not expected to write completely faultless English and will not be penalized for minor errors, provided these do not impede the communication of the message.

The markscheme used to assess PET Writing Part 2 is given below. (To see how the markscheme operates, refer to the **Examples of student writing** on pages 57–60 and in the sample answers on the CD-ROM.) It is used in conjunction with a task-specific markscheme. (The **Keys to Practice Tests 1 and 2** on pages 48 and 49 include examples of task-specific markschemes for PET Writing Part 2, as do the keys to the Writing tests on the CD-ROM.)

PET Part 2: Markscheme

5	All content elements covered appropriately. Message clearly communicated to reader.
4	All content elements adequately dealt with. Message communicated successfully, on the whole.
3	All content elements attempted. Message requires some effort by the reader. OR One content element omitted but others clearly communicated.
2	Two content elements omitted, or unsuccessfully dealt with. Message only partly communicated to reader. OR Script may be slightly short (20–25 words)
1	Little relevant content and/or message requires excessive effort by the reader, or short (10–19 words)
0	Totally irrelevant or totally incomprehensible or too short (under 10 words).

In PET Writing Part 3, the student has the choice of writing either an informal letter or a story. The focus of the assessment in this part is on the student's ability to control a range of structures and vocabulary, and to organize his/her ideas coherently. To receive a band 5 score (13 to 15 marks) a student has to show good control of grammar, word order, vocabulary, spelling and punctuation. It doesn't matter if there are some mistakes, as long as these don't cause misunderstanding. Important words in the descriptions of a band 5 piece of writing are 'confident and ambitious use of language'. This means that to score highly a student must use a wide range of structures and vocabulary and attempt some complex sentence patterns, such as relative clauses, time clauses, conditionals, comparatives, and clauses with *because* or *although*. Where appropriate, sentences should be joined using simple linking words or phrases, such as *first*, *next*, *so*, *but*, *in fact*, *best of all*, so that it is easy for the reader to follow the ideas in the letter or story. The markscheme used to assess Part 3 is given opposite. Band 5 represents a score of 13 to 15 marks. Band 4 represents 10 to 12 marks, and so on. For examples of how the markscheme operates, refer to the **Examples of student writing** on pages 57–60 and on the CD-ROM.

While students are developing their writing skills during the preparation course, it is advisable to use a less formal approach to assessment. The emphasis should be on communicating meaning. Students should be awarded marks for successfully conveying their ideas to the reader. If the teacher pays too much attention to the correctness of language forms, the student's writing fluency will be inhibited. However, students should be encouraged to check their own work for language errors, especially in those areas where they frequently make mistakes. For example, they should make sure they haven't used the present tense when a past tense is required, and they should check that they haven't used an incorrect preposition.

Assessment of speaking

In the Speaking paper, students are assessed on how well they can speak and communicate, rather than on the content of what they say or their personality. They should, however, be prepared to speak to their partner(s) and develop a conversation appropriately. As the test aims to assess spontaneous, communicative language skills, prepared speeches are not acceptable; nor are one-word answers. Students should be ready to express their views and opinions in response to the tasks set, and to respond naturally to their partner's contributions.

Marks are awarded on five different scales:

1 **Grammar and vocabulary**: The accurate use of an appropriate range of grammar is assessed, along with the candidate's vocabulary resource.

PET Part 3: Markscheme

Band 5 Very good attempt:

- Confident and ambitious use of language
- Wide range of structures and vocabularly within the task set
- Well organized and coherent, through use of simple linking devices
- Errors are minor, due to ambition and non-impeding

Requires no effort by the reader

Band 4 Good attempt:

- Fairly ambitious use of language
- More than adequate range of structures and vocabulary within the task set
- Evidence of organization and some linking of sentences
- Some errors, generally non-impeding

Requires only a little effort by the reader

Band 3 Adequate attempt:

- Language is unambitious, or if ambitious, flawed
- Adequate range of structures and vocabulary
- Some attempt at organization; linking of sentences not always maintained
- A number of errors may be present, but are mostly non-impeding

Requires some effort by the reader

Band 2 Inadequate attempt:

- Language is simplistic / limited / repetitive
- Inadequate range of structures and vocabulary
- Some incoherence; erratic punctuation
- Numerous errors, which sometimes impede communication

Requires considerable effort by the reader

Band 1 Poor attempt:

- Severely restricted command of language
- No evidence of range of structures and vocabulary
- Seriously incoherent; absence of punctuation
- Very poor control; difficult to understand

Requires excessive effort by the reader

0   Achieves nothing:

- Language impossible to understand or totally irrelevant to task.

2. **Discourse management**: The candidate's ability to produce extended utterances and a coherent flow of language is assessed.
3. **Pronunciation**: The candidate's ability to produce comprehensible utterances is assessed.
4. **Interactive communication**: The candidate's ability to take part in tasks is assessed. The examiner will look for evidence that the candidate can initiate a conversation with a partner and respond appropriately to him or her, with reasonable fluency.
5. **Global achievement**: This reflects the candidate's overall contribution and level of language competence.

When giving students feedback on their spoken English, remember that fluency and confidence are important in the examination. Students who are inhibited by fear of making mistakes, or who misunderstand the aim of the tasks, may be at a disadvantage. Teachers should explain to students that the ability to communicate naturally and meaningfully is what is being assessed. Encourage them, therefore, to become involved immediately with tasks, to say what they are thinking, and to work co-operatively with their partner. Advice about each part of the Speaking test, and how it is assessed, can be found in the following sections of the Coursebook:

Speaking Part 1: Unit 1, Lesson 1
Speaking Part 2: Unit 2, Lesson 1
Speaking Part 3: Unit 6, Lesson 2
Speaking Part 4: Unit 7, Lesson 1
Revision: Unit 10, Lesson 2

Information about the Speaking test is also available in corresponding sections of this book.

An additional resource is the **Sample speaking test**, which is recorded on the course Audio CD. Refer to page 53 of this book for suggestions on how to make use of this sample test.

How to use *Ready for PET*

Ready for PET has ten units with two lessons in each unit. Each lesson is topic based. This is because it is important for students to develop a range of vocabulary to deal at a simple level with a number of everyday topics. Units 1–8 focus on giving information and advice about one particular test task; Units 9 and 10 revise this material. Each unit aims to develop the four skills of reading, writing, listening and speaking. There are vocabulary revision and extension exercises, and exercises practising the grammatical patterns needed for PET in each unit. In this way, *Ready for PET* gives students comprehensive test preparation.

Ready for PET is designed for use with the students' general English coursebook. *Ready for PET* can be used in a variety of ways, depending on the amount of time available in class and for homework. The teacher may want to include work from *Ready for PET* in regular class time, or devote a separate class specifically to test preparation.

There will be many instances when work in *Ready for PET* complements work in the students' general coursebook, for example in terms of topic or skills development.

The lessons in *Ready for PET* do not have to be followed in numerical order; nor does every task have to be completed. The teacher should select and organize tasks according to the needs of students. However, the **Get ready** box and its accompanying exercise, found in every lesson, should never be overlooked. In the **Get ready** boxes, students are given specific advice on different parts of the test. The **Get ready** boxes should be used with the charts on pages 2–3 of the Coursebook. The student will then acquire an overview of the whole test, together with detailed information about its separate parts.

Some exercises in *Ready for PET* can be left out if the teacher is short of time, but the speaking and writing tasks are essential. Students generally need a lot of practice to develop fluency in these skills at this level. As they have to do the PET Speaking test with another student, they need to practise with a partner in class. There are suggestions in this book on how to organize individual speaking activities. If there is not enough time to do the writing tasks in class, they can be set for homework. However, it is worth spending a short time preparing the activity in class. The aim of any preparation activity should be to stimulate ideas, activate essential vocabulary, and make sure that students understand the writing task instructions. Ask students to check their written work themselves before they hand it to you.

If there is no class time available for test preparation, students can use *Ready for PET* for self study, with their teacher's guidance. If this is the case, they should read pages 2–4 of the Coursebook carefully before they start. The teacher should help them to work out a study timetable, and check at intervals that they are keeping to it. It may be helpful for these students to use the 'with key' edition of *Ready for PET*, so that they can check their work. Alternatively, you may want to make the key available to them only after they have completed the exercises in a lesson, or you may prefer to check their work yourself. It will help students if you check what they write in the writing tasks. Self-study students will also need encouragement to organize speaking activities with another student.

The tests on the CD-ROM can be used by all students in their own time at regular intervals to practise test tasks and to monitor their own progress. You should make sure that all students complete a timed practice test before the real test. If possible, organize this in quite a formal way, with a teacher invigilating, operating the CD player for the Listening test, and asking the questions and giving the instructions in the Speaking test.

The lesson notes that follow give detailed help with each of the lessons in *Ready for PET*.

1.1 Personal information

Topic

The topic of this lesson is personal information. The ability to talk about oneself and give information in both formal and informal situations is one of the principal skills expected of a PET student. By the time students are at PET level, they should be able to:

- give personal information spontaneously, in real-life spoken contexts (PET Speaking Part 1);
- spell any part of their name (PET Speaking Part 1).

Lesson focus

The focus of this lesson is PET Speaking Part 1, and most time should be spent on this activity.

1 Writing

This activity introduces the vocabulary of personal information and provides a lead-in to the type of information students may need to give in PET Speaking Part 1.

Read through the form with the students and make sure that they understand the prompts. Afterwards, check that they have written down appropriate information about themselves.

2 Listening 1.1

1 Students listen to the Audio CD and note down the information. If necessary, stop the CD and play the track again. Then go through the information with the whole class.

Ask students to think about how the information is presented, and then ask them how this differs from their own culture.

KEY

A Name: John
Surname: Rose
Home town: London
E-mail address: john@webmail.net
Mobile number: 02227 813000
Sex: Male
Age: 16
Interests: Football, tennis, volleyball, listening to music, watching television

B Name: Amanda
Surname: Wilson
Home town: York
E-mail address: amanda@webmail.net
Mobile number: 02227 963214
Sex: Female
Age: 17
Interests: Horse riding and hill walking

RECORDING SCRIPT

A Hello. My name is John, that's J-O-H-N. And my surname is Rose, that's R-O-S-E. I would like to give you some information about myself. First of all, I live in London and my e-mail address is: john@webmail.net. Or you can get me on my mobile, the number is: 02227 813000. So, what else can I tell you? I'm a 16-year-old boy and so I'm still at school and I'm very interested in sport. I'm quite good at football and I also enjoy playing tennis and volleyball. When I'm not playing sport, I like listening to music and watching television.

B Hello. My name's Amanda Wilson and you spell my first name A-M-A-N-D-A, Amanda, and my surname is Wilson, which is spelt W-I-L-S-O-N. My name's not really difficult to spell, but people always seem to make mistakes in it! I live in York, that's Y-O-R-K. and my e-mail address is: amanda@webmail.net. I've got a mobile phone, but I don't use it that much. The number is: 02227 963214. So, what can I tell you about myself? Well, I'm a 17-year-old English girl and I work as a shop assistant in a large shop in my home city. In my free time, I like to get out of the city, however, and I'm very interested in horse riding and hill walking. I'm not very good at horse riding yet because I only started last year, but I've been hill walking since I was 12 years old. I love it!

2 The follow-up task gives students revision and practice of question forms. This is essential for PET Speaking Parts 2 and 4.

First, check that the students are able to make the correct question forms. Then do any remedial grammar work that may be necessary on question formation. Once students have made their questions and you have checked them, ask them to look at the activities in the box in **exercise 3.1**.

3 Speaking

1 Students work individually, ordering the activities in the box from most interesting (1) to least interesting (12). Then, in pairs, they give the reasons for their choices. Elicit what they have found out about their partners and monitor for errors in question forms.

2 Giving students practice in accurate spelling is essential for Part 1 of the Speaking test. Revise letters of the alphabet with them, and then encourage students to spell their names out loud, giving help with pronunciation where necessary.

3 1.2 After students have listened to the recording, check their answers and deal with any problems of alphabet or transcription.

Go through the **Get ready** box with the students, which prepares them for PET Speaking Part 1. Answer any questions and remind them that, although they will be examined with a partner, they will need to answer the examiner's questions directly in Part 1 of the test.

Play Part 1 of the Sample speaking test on the course Audio CD to the students and ask them:

- how many questions each person is asked;
- what type of questions they are asked.

In groups of three, ask students to practise the conversation, taking turns to be the examiner. They should give real information about themselves and make up some questions of their own, based on the ideas in point 1 of the **Get ready** box.

KEY

3 1 Yolanda Brown
   2 Yusuf Amiri
   3 Angela Beaufort
   4 Paolo Mitchell
   5 Irina Gallagher

RECORDING SCRIPT
1 My name is Yolanda Brown, that's Y O L A N D A B R O W N. 2 My name is Yusuf Amiri, that's Y U S U F A M I R I. 3 My name is Angela Beaufort, that's A N G E L A B E A U F O R T. 4 My name is Paolo Mitchell, that's P A O L O M I T C H E L L. 5 My name is Irina Gallagher, that's I R I N A G A L L A G H E R.

4 Writing

This task practises the grammar in PET Writing Part 1. **Unit 8**, **Lesson 2** also deals with Part 1 of the Writing paper. If students are unfamiliar with transformation exercises, do the first example with them as a model.

KEY
1 good football 2 interested in 3 old are 4 do you 5 you spell

5 Writing

The writing task may be set for homework. Discuss the Internet context and the likely reader first. Point out that language can be fairly informal in this case.

6 Listening 1.3

1 Ask the students to look at the dialogue and try to decide which of the phrases best completes each gap. Point out that some of the phrases do not fit at all. Elicit the answers from the students and also their reasons for each choice.

KEY
1 C 2 E 3 F 4 B 5 G

2 Let the students listen to the Audio CD to check their answers.

KEY
A, D

RECORDING SCRIPT
David: Hello. I'm David. **Victoria:** Hi. I'm Victoria. I'm a friend of Tom's from college. **David:** Yes, I'm one of his friends too, and we play football together. What do you study? **Victoria:** I'm doing languages. What about you? **David:** I've finished college, actually, and I'm working as a windsurfing instructor.

Victoria: Oh, I'm really interested in watersports, but I'm not very good at windsurfing.

David: That doesn't matter. You could learn.

Victoria: Yes, I suppose so. But what I'm really interested in is sailing.

David: So am I. I'm running a course which starts next week. Would you be interested in joining?

Victoria: Oh … I might be … it depends.

3 Ask students, in pairs or small groups, to discuss the three focus questions. After a few minutes, ask for their views and begin a class discussion about the nature of social conversation.

7 Reading

1 This task helps with PET Reading Part 1. Both notices introduce vocabulary which will be important later. Make sure that students understand what BLOCK CAPITALS are.

KEY
1 B   2 C

2 Explain that a signature is how you write your name with a pen, on official documents.

Tell students that in the exam, their names will be printed on their answer sheets and they will be asked to sign to confirm that their details are correct. The word *'signature'* indicates the place where they are to do this.

A regular thing

Topic

The topic of this lesson is daily life and the ordinary things we do regularly. Reading and listening texts in PET often feature people speaking about their everyday lives and activities. Students should be prepared to write or talk about their own daily activities in PET Writing Parts 2 and 3, and in PET Speaking Parts 1 and 4.

Lesson focus

The focus of this lesson is how to do PET Writing Part 2, and most time should be spent on this activity.

1 Vocabulary

1 This matching activity revises and extends students' vocabulary about their everyday lives, and introduces the lesson topic. If students work in pairs or groups they can share vocabulary.

KEY
attend: class, meeting
boil: water
brush: hair, pet, shoes, teeth
clean: desk, furniture, shoes, teeth
comb: hair
dial: number
dust: desk, furniture
feed: pet
iron: shirt
miss: bus, class, meeting
tidy: desk, dishes, hair
tie: hair, shoelaces
wash: dishes, hair, pet, shirt

2 The second matching activity focuses on common phrasal verbs. Students are not expected to be familiar with a wide range of phrasal verbs at PET level, but they should be aware that they exist. This may help them to understand some of the more difficult sections of the reading texts.

After each of the matching tasks students have the opportunity to talk about their own regular activities and revise the use of adverbs of frequency and other frequency expressions. Give them examples to help them:

I sometimes miss the bus to school.
I put on make-up before I go out in the evening.

> **KEY**
>
> **hand in**: books, homework
> **join in**: game
> **take off**: make-up, socks
> **put on**: light, make-up, music, radio, socks
> **put up**: umbrella
> **put away**: books, game, homework, make-up, socks, umbrella
> **plug in**: light, radio
> **turn up**: light, music, radio
> **turn on**: light, music, radio

2 Reading

These short messages are examples of the type students are asked to write in PET Writing Part 2. The task provides students with models of the kinds of message they may have to write, and familiarizes them with the instructions for this part (eg, *thank, describe,* etc). Elicit the types of short message students might write in their daily lives, eg a telephone message or a note about homework.

Point out to students that in each of these messages it is clear who the message is to and from.

> **KEY**
>
> 1 A, B   2 C   3 A   4 C   5 A   6 B, C   7 B   8 A

3 Writing

In PET Writing Part 2, students write a short message (35–45 words), closely following the instructions given. There are up to 5 marks available for this part, depending on how successfully the student has communicated the three points in the instructions. Minor language errors will not be penalized, as long as the message is clear. For more information about how PET Writing Part 2 is assessed, refer to pages 5–6 and 57–60.

1   Put the students into pairs. In this case, paired students should *not* be sitting next to each other. Students should write the note, making sure they cover all three points given in the instructions. Remind them that they have just read examples of people explaining, suggesting and offering in the previous reading activity. Remind them also to address their classmate (eg 'Dear X', 'Hi Y'), and to sign their name at the end. Encourage them to keep within the word limit given (35–45 words).

2   Students exchange notes with their partners. Ask them to check first of all that their partners have covered all three points in the instructions. Ignore language errors which don't interfere with understanding the message at this stage. Students should then write a reply to their partners, exchange notes and check them as before. Go through the **Get ready** box with the students.

3   Students can do this for homework.

> **KEY**
>
> Students' messages won't be exactly like these, but they should contain the three points given in the instructions.
>
> **Model message:**
> Dear Alice,
> Thank you very much for helping me with my homework last week. My teacher said it was much better than usual! Can you come to my house again on Saturday afternoon? This time I'll help you with your Italian.
> Love,
> Daniela
>
> **Model message:**
> Ben,
> Your mother phoned to say she has posted you the books you asked for. It's a very heavy parcel. When it arrives, you should check she has sent the right books because she wasn't sure exactly which ones you wanted.
> Bruno

4 Writing

Students at this level should already know the different types of comparison clauses given here, but will probably need reminding of them. Point out that the meaning doesn't change when certain alternative structures are used.

This type of sentence transformation is found in PET Writing Part 1. Point out that students may have to write one, two or three words (never more).

> **KEY**
>
> 1 as tidy as
> 2 faster than
> 3 more comfortable than
> 4 less homework than
> 5 worse than

5 Reading

This activity practises PET Reading Part 5. It extends the topic of daily life, as students have to think about inventions which have changed people's lives.

> **KEY**
>
> 1 A   2 B   3 D   4 A   5 C
> 6 C   7 B   8 D   9 A   10 B

2.1 You live and learn

Topic

The topic of this lesson is education. Education is a frequent topic in all parts of the examination because most PET candidates are full-time students. Tasks in PET Speaking Part 2 are often set in the context of school or college.

Lesson focus

The main focus of this lesson is the preparation of students for PET Speaking Part 2. Most time should be spent on this activity.

1 Vocabulary

1 The purpose of this activity is to get students used to talking about photographs. It introduces some key vocabulary and the topic of education in the broadest sense. Students work individually and then discuss their answers in pairs. Once they have exchanged their ideas, go through the activity with the whole class. Alternatively, build up a list of vocabulary on the board with the class first, and then let them work individually or in pairs.

2 This activity encourages students to look at photographs for specific details.

2 Speaking

1 Students should use the photographs and discuss their ideas in pairs. Encourage the students to work through all the ideas systematically. They should consider all the possibilities of each idea before coming to a conclusion. This is good practice for PET Speaking Part 2 and PET Speaking Part 4.

2 1.4 This task consolidates the students' spoken work by asking them to follow a similar text and understand its outcome. Students should discuss their answers in pairs before they are given the correct answer. Ask them why they think Polly likes studying in this way.

KEY

Her favourite way of studying Spanish is alone with a text book.
B is the correct picture.
She likes studying in this way because she's good at grammar, and the book has got lots of practice exercises.

RECORDING SCRIPT

Boy: Hello, Polly. How are your Spanish classes going?

Polly: Oh, OK. The teacher's very nice, but the classes are a bit boring. I really like studying on my own, you know. My dad bought me a Spanish CD for my computer, but actually I prefer the textbook because I'm good at grammar, and the book has got lots of practice exercises. One day, I'd like to be able to listen and understand the words to Spanish pop music, but I'm not good enough for that yet!

3 This task builds on the question-writing activities in **Unit 1 Lesson 1** and provides further practice in question formation. This is a central element of the PET Speaking test. Students should write questions in the second person, as if they were talking to Polly. They should be checked for accuracy. Elicit questions from the class and put these on the board, showing different ways of asking the same question where appropriate.

3 Speaking

1 This exercise prepares students for PET Speaking Part 2. In this part of the test, the examiner describes an imaginary situation to the candidates and gives them a sheet of visual prompts. The instructions are read twice and then students perform the task without help. They have approximately two minutes to discuss the situation and arrive at some kind of conclusion. Marks are given for language used and interactive strategies employed, rather than for ideas. It doesn't matter if students don't finish the task, as long as they make a good attempt at it. The task does *not* have one right answer; it is designed to create a discussion.

Read the **Get ready** box before students attempt the task. Check that they understand the visuals and pre-teach any vocabulary. Monitor for problems, but avoid giving feedback on language errors at this stage.

2 Ask students to look at the dialogue and complete the task. Elicit answers, with reasons.

KEY

1 F 2 E 3 G 4 C 5 A

3 1.5 Ask the students which two phrases weren't used. Play the Audio CD so that they can check their answers.

KEY

B D

RECORDING SCRIPT

Valerie: So, our friend wants to learn a new language?

Pietro: That's right, and he's only got £20 to spend, so he can't buy all these things, can he?

Valerie: No, he can't. Let's start by talking about which of them will be useful for him.

Pietro: OK, then afterwards we can decide which one he should buy.

Valerie: OK. Shall we start with this one, the dictionary?

Pietro: Yes, I think he should buy one of those, because it's very useful if you don't know what words mean.

Valerie: Yes, I agree, and it's also good for checking spelling. But what about a textbook? They're useful too.

Pietro: Yes they are, but maybe he won't need one because he'll have a teacher.

Valerie: Possibly. Or he may get one free when he pays for the course.

Pietro: Oh yes, that's a good point.

4 Listening 1.6

This listening task practises PET Listening Part 4. Ask for answers to the questions, with reasons.

KEY
1 B 2 B 3 A 4 B 5 A

RECORDING SCRIPT

Tim: Hi Janet. How's your computer course going?

Janet: Oh, I've just had my class, actually. We have them twice a week and each one lasts two hours.

Tim: Gosh. That's long. Doesn't it get boring?

Janet: Well, you need that long to actually do a whole document. It's really good because I can do all sorts of things on my computer that I never even knew existed before.

Tim: I can't say the same for my cookery course.

Janet: Oh, Tim, why not? I thought you were enjoying it.

Tim: Oh it's enjoyable enough, but we just don't seem to make much progress. We spent the whole of last week's lesson learning how to fry an egg.

Janet: Well, it's not an easy thing to do properly, you know.

Tim: Oh I know, but I don't even like eggs.

Janet: Oh poor Tim! So … how often is it?

Tim: Just once a week, for an hour and a half.

Janet: And do you get to eat all the things you make?

Tim: Well, you're not meant to eat them there, but you can take them home because you have to buy all the stuff in the first place. It's cakes next week.

Janet: Oh, that sounds fun.

Tim: Oh yes. I'm looking forward to it. But Janet, I wanted to ask you something, actually. Have you learnt how to send e-mails on your course yet?

Janet: Oh yes, we did that in the first week.

Tim: Because I can't get my computer to send them properly, and I was wondering if you'd show me how it's done?

Janet: Well, if you bring me one of your cakes, I suppose I could try.

Tim: Great, well, when I've made them…

5 Writing

These sentence transformations may be set for homework.

KEY
1 is two hours
2 much does
3 in my
4 with
5 about talking

2 All the best books

Topic

The topic of this lesson is books and reading. This topic may be the focus of a PET reading or listening text, especially a PET Reading Part 2 or Part 4 text. Students should be prepared to write or speak about their own reading preferences in PET Writing Part 3, and in the Speaking paper.

Lesson focus

The focus of this lesson is how to do PET Reading Part 2, and most time should be spent on this activity. A secondary focus is writing a story, which students may do in PET Writing Part 3.

1 Reading

This activity is an introduction to the topic and should be done quite quickly. Read through the information with the students and give them time to write down their answers. They can discuss them with a partner first, and then with the class.

KEY
a) 2   b) 1
a) 1   b) 2
1 C   2 B

2 Vocabulary

This activity provides students with vocabulary to talk about different types of books. They may have to do this in PET Speaking Part 2 or Part 4.

Check first that the students understand what each type of book is. Then let them work with a partner to do the activity and answer the questions. Go through the answers afterwards, with the whole class.

The vocabulary in this activity can also be applied to different types of films and videos. Students can talk about videos rather than books in the follow-up questions, if they want to.

KEY
A travel
B romance
C humour
D mystery
E biography
F thriller
G horror
H science fiction

3 Reading

This task prepares students for PET Reading Part 2, which tests their understanding of factual texts in detail. Students read profiles of five people and then match each profile to one short text chosen from eight.

In the example here, the eight short texts are advertisements for different books. The short texts could also be descriptions of different holiday destinations, television programmes, leisure activities, etc.

Students must read the five people profiles and the eight short texts carefully to find the correct matches. There is only one correct answer for each question. However, there is also at least one attractive (but wrong) possible answer for each question, to tempt students.

You can ask students to go through either the reading task or the questions in the **Get ready** box first. The **Get ready** box helps students through the reading activity in stages, and is useful if they are unfamiliar with this type of exercise.

KEY
1 C   2 E   3 B   4 A   5 G

KEY TO **GET READY** BOX
2 C and F
No. A is a novel for teenagers and adults; B is an autobiography for adults; E is a science fiction story for teenagers. C or F may be suitable. C is for very young children and F is for children between five and ten years old.
3 C is about animals. F is about space travel.
4 F is unsuitable because it is factual, and not a story that Laura can read to her grandson many times. The most suitable book is C, because it is for young children and it's about animals.

4 Vocabulary

This picks out a particular type of word formation used in one of the short texts. Ask students to find other expressions in the text which are useful when talking about books (or films).

Examples:
an exciting novel, thrilling action, a realistic picture.

Now look at the sentences in **1–5** and complete them as a whole class activity. Check that the answers are sensible before you write them on the board.

5 Writing

In PET Writing Part 3, students are given a choice of topic. They may either write a letter or a story. The activities here prepare students for the story-writing option. (There is practice in writing letters in **lessons 4.1, 6.1, 8.1** and **9.2**.)

When they write stories, students are not expected to show sophisticated story-telling skills. However, they should be able to write a coherent narrative, and they will get credit for successfully using a range of grammar and vocabulary. They should, for example, be able to handle past tenses, attempt some complex sentence patterns using time clauses and relative clauses, and use linking words, such as *first, next* and *so*. They should also be able to use a variety of appropriate words when telling their stories, and not have to resort to unnecessary repetition. As stimulus for their stories, students are either given the title of a story, as here, or the first sentence. Stories may be fictional, like this one, or they may relate to students' personal experiences.

1 Do this as a whole-class activity, or ask students to do it in pairs or small groups and then check answers with the whole class. You could have the story, with the sentences in the correct order, written on an OHT and reveal it line by line, as students decide which sentence comes next. Alternatively, you could give students photocopies of the correctly ordered story, or get them to write out a correct version for themselves. They will need it as a model for their own story, which they write later. The activity should draw students' attention to some of the features which make a story coherent, eg use of pronouns.

Encourage the students to answer the questions in **2** about the story (*'Who does the visitor come to see?'* etc). Point out it is always important to know *who* the story is about (Jenny) and *where* ('home', 'at her front door') and *when* ('One day when Jenny arrived home') the story happens. It's also often important to know how the character *feels* ('surprise'), and to have some kind of *ending* to the story ('*She went inside, took out her homework and studied all evening.*').

Ask students to underline all the past tense verbs in the story. Correct use of past tenses is a feature of writing narratives.

Ask the students to indicate the linking words and phrases in the story which help to organize the ideas, and make the story clear ('*One day when*', '*this person*', '*although*', '*when*', '*that day*', '*and*').

Point out to students that stories are often more dramatic if there is some direct speech in them. Make sure they know the correct punctuation for direct speech in English, as shown in this story. Also ask them if this story could be divided into more than one paragraph. A second paragraph could begin at '*She knew what she had to do.*'

2 Brainstorming answers to questions like these will help students to develop their own stories. They can make up a story or tell one based on their personal experience. Get them to think up answers to the questions in pairs.

3 Students may then collaborate to write one story per pair or group, or write stories individually for homework. Encourage them to keep to the word limit of about 100 words. When the stories are written, ask students to look at their own, or someone else's story, and to see if they can improve it. Ask them these questions:

- Is it clear who the story is about, and where and when it happened?
- Are any feelings mentioned?
- Can the organization of the ideas in the story, or the sequence of events, be improved by adding linking words like *when, after, because, so, although, in order to, first, next, suddenly, in the end*?
- Is the language used as interesting and varied as possible? For example, can any repetition be taken out, or any different adjectives be added?

Finally, ask students to check the stories for errors of grammar (especially verb tenses), spelling and punctuation. Completed stories can be read out or put on a class noticeboard. For more information about how PET Writing Part 3 is assessed, refer to pages 5–6 and 57–60.

KEY

1 **The Strange Visitor**
One day when Jenny arrived home, she saw someone standing at her front door, hidden underneath a large, old-fashioned coat and hat. She didn't know why, but she felt this person was very old, wise and kind. Although the person didn't speak, Jenny could hear some words in her head. 'This is only my first visit, and when we meet again I will show you my home on a distant planet. To prepare for that day, you must study hard and learn all you can.' Jenny cried out in surprise and the strange visitor disappeared. She knew what she had to do. She went inside, took out her homework and studied all evening.

3 1 Holiday adventures

Topic

The topic of this lesson is travel and holidays. Students should be prepared to speak and write about their own holiday experiences.

Lesson focus

The focus of this lesson is how to do PET Reading Part 3, and most time should be spent on this activity.

1 Reading

This is an introduction to the topic and should be dealt with quickly. It gives practice in reading and understanding notices and also revises essential topic vocabulary (*travel agency, excursion, package holiday, reservation, luggage, booking*, etc).

Students can work individually or in pairs. Once they have written down their answers, go through them with the class. Read each notice out to the class and discuss the possible choices of answer for each. Ask students for their reasons.

KEY
a) 2   b) 3   c) 1
1 C   2 B   3 A

2 Speaking

1   This activity gives students practice in talking about photographs (PET Speaking Part 3). They should answer the questions about photograph A using the vocabulary in the box.

2   Students should now describe the picture, using ideas from **exercise 2.1**.

3   Students follow the same process to build up a description of photograph B. They should remember to:

- say where the photograph was taken
- describe any people in it
- say what they are doing
- mention things they can see
- suggest what the people are feeling, talking about, have just done, or are going to do.

KEY
1   1 a young woman
2 in her bedroom
3 packing a suitcase
4 a plastic suitcase, clothes, a bed, a quilt
5 excited about her holiday; and nervous, because she doesn't know what will happen.
2   **Model answer:**
This picture shows a young woman in her bedroom. She's packing some things in a plastic suitcase, which is on her bed. There are some clothes already in the suitcase and some more on the bed. The bed has a pink-and-white quilt and a pillow on it. I think the young woman is going abroad on holiday so she probably feels excited, but perhaps she also feels nervous because she doesn't know what's going to happen.
Extra details may also be given.
The young woman has long dark hair and she's wearing jeans and a green T-shirt. The bedroom is quite small and doesn't have much furniture apart from the bed. There may be a cupboard in the room but I can't quite see.

3 Reading

This prepares students for PET Reading Part 3. The texts in this part of the Reading paper are the longest in the test. In them, students have to scan a text for specific information, usually of a practical nature. The questions come *before* the text, so students should read them first and then scan the text to find each answer. There will be some redundant information in the text and students will come across some unfamiliar words. Students need to develop strategies for guessing the meaning of important words. For example, they should get into the habit of trying to work out the meaning of a word from its context, seeing if other words near it have a similar or opposite meaning, and looking at the formation of the word. Ask: *Is it a compound of other known words? Does it have a known prefix or suffix? Is it similar to a word in the students' own language?*, etc.

1   Students should skim-read the text to get a general idea of the meaning and to see whether the scuba-diving holiday it describes sounds attractive. Check that they can name the animals shown in the photos.

2   The points in the **Get ready** box help students develop useful exam strategies. They can read through the box either before or after they decide whether the sentences are correct or incorrect.

Students may work individually or in pairs, using their own strategies. Before checking answers, go through the points in the **Get ready** box. Ask students to compare their strategies with the ones suggested in the box, and see if they want to revise any of their answers in the light of them.

Alternatively, you can go through the points in the **Get ready** box and answer the questions on the text at the same time, as a whole class activity.

KEY		
1 Incorrect	2 Correct	3 Incorrect
4 Correct	5 Incorrect	6 Incorrect
7 Correct	8 Incorrect	9 Correct
10 Correct		

KEY TO GET READY BOX

2   **Sentence 6**: Diving opportunities
       Sentence 7: The accommodation
       Sentence 9: Additional land tours
       Sentence 10: Prices and booking

3   **Sentence 1**: *giant tortoises that can reach 120 years in age*
       Sentence 2: *The Galapagos are also home to penguins (nowhere else are they found so far north)*
       Sentence 3: *at certain times of year, whales pass by the islands*
       Sentence 4: *The wildlife and scenery is so varied here that a seven-day voyage is the minimum you should consider*

4   No   Yes

4 Writing

Students at this level should have command of simple time clauses, but will probably need to revise them. Point out that the meaning doesn't change when certain alternative structures are used.

This type of sentence transformation is found in PET Writing Part 1. Students will also gain marks for using simple time clauses in PET Writing Part 3, and in the Speaking paper.

KEY

1 you have learnt
2 soon as
3 we have/we've
4 was on holiday
5 before you book

5 Vocabulary

Describing holidays is common in PET Writing Part 3 and in PET Speaking Part 4. Students should be prepared to talk about their own holiday experiences and preferences. Encourage them to add more words to each category.

KEY

Transport: car, plane, coach, train
Accommodation: hotel, guest house, tent
Scenery: beach, countryside
Activities: swimming, taking photos, sunbathing, picnics
Things to pack: sunglasses, suntan lotion, guidebook
souvenirs: postcards, shells, handicrafts

6 Speaking

This practises the kind of task in PET Speaking Part 4.

Students should use the words in the previous vocabulary activity and aim to have a conversation for about three minutes about holidays they like and don't like. They should talk about holiday destinations, activities, companions, the weather, and anything else they consider important. The teacher monitors the conversations and, after three minutes, gives feedback.

3.2 Just the job

Topic

The topic of this lesson is work and jobs. Students should be prepared to discuss their job plans, or real jobs if they have them, in PET Writing Part 3 and in the Speaking paper.

Lesson focus

The focus of this lesson is PET Listening Part 2, and most time should be spent on this activity.

1 Reading

This kind of question is found in PET Reading Part 1. It is a warm-up activity here, and should be done quickly. Its purpose is to introduce the topic and revise some key 'job' vocabulary, eg *staff*.

2 Vocabulary

1–2 These revise and extend key vocabulary and draw attention to word formation patterns in English. If students are aware of word formation patterns, they may be able to work out the meanings of unknown words in reading texts. Students work in pairs so they can share their knowledge. Ask them to complete or check their answers by consulting a dictionary.

KEY		
1	Profession	Subject studied
	architect	architecture
	doctor	medicine
	lawyer	law
	artist	art
	cook	cookery/cooking
	engineer	engineering
	tourist guide	tourism
	hairdresser	hairdressing
	journalist	journalism
	businesswoman	business
	actor	acting
	chemist	chemistry
	biologist	biology
	physicist	physics
	musician	music

2	Verb	Noun
	apply	application
	organize	organization
	qualify	qualification
	decide	decision
	operate	operation
	employ	employment
	advertise	advertisement
	govern	government
	manage	management
	retire	retirement
	insure	insurance
	succeed	success

3 Listening 1.7–1.10

This listening activity practises PET Listening Part 3, where students have to listen and complete some notes. It also gives practice in PET Listening Part 1, where students have to choose one of three pictures.

1 Students should listen to the Audio CD at least twice. They will hear four different women talking about their jobs. This is a note-taking exercise, so play each text as many times as they need to complete the table. Pause if necessary, and use the illustrations as visual prompts.

KEY
Speaker 1: uniform, car, city centre, controlling traffic
Speaker 2: jeans, computer, advertising agency, drawing.
Speaker 3: white coat, microscope, zoo, testing.
Speaker 4: suit, phone, bank, helping customers
1 C   2 A   3 D   4 B

RECORDING SCRIPT
1 I love what I do and I'm very proud of the uniform I wear. I drive around for most of the day but I'm always somewhere in the city centre. My job is controlling the traffic. When I hear there's a traffic problem I go and see what I can do about it. I just use my hands and my voice – no equipment's necessary – except for my car, of course. I couldn't work without that!

18

2 I never did well at school. I was only interested in drawing – I was quite good at that. And that's what I do now – drawing. I work in an advertising agency and I do the artwork for advertisements. But I don't use a pencil or paint – it's all done on a computer – that's the only piece of equipment I need. I like being comfortable when I work, so I wear jeans. I don't even own a suit.

3 This is my first job and I've only been here for a year. My microscope is my most important piece of equipment. I couldn't do my work here in the zoo without it. I love animals, but I don't often get to see the ones here! My job is testing. I test all kinds of things – the animals' food, the water they drink, and if they get ill, I test their blood. It's very important that everything here is clean, so I have to wear a white coat over my clothes, and I'm always washing my hands!

4 Actually, I want to change what I do. I work in a bank, and it's a good job, but I'd like to do something more exciting. Here it's the same thing every day. My job is helping customers. I help customers when they come into the bank and I help them when they phone up. I don't really have any equipment apart from the phone. I spend a lot of time on the phone. I have to wear a suit at work, which I hate – I'd much prefer to wear jeans!

2 1.11 This activity prepares students for PET Listening Part 2. The listening text in this part of the paper consists of one person speaking, or a dialogue between two people. The context is usually a radio programme, or someone addressing a group of students, tourists, etc. The multiple-choice questions focus on factual information in the listening text. Students should try to read the questions through once before the recording begins. It is important that they keep up with the questions when the Audio CD is playing; this means they should not spend too long on the answer to any one question.

Tell the students they are going to listen to a woman, Amanda Turner, talking on the radio about her job, and that they must answer some multiple-choice questions. Let them look at the questions quickly so that they get an idea about what kind of information they are going to hear and what they should listen out for.

Draw attention to the points in the **Get ready** box and then play the recording all the way through. Students should answer as many questions as they can. Ask students to compare their answers and discuss any difficulties without revealing the correct answers. Play the recording again and see if students are now more confident about their answers. Check answers and, if necessary, play all or parts of the recording again, or refer students to the relevant parts of the Recording Script.

KEY

1 C   2 B   3 C   4 B   5 A   6 A

RECORDING SCRIPT

Presenter: … and today in our series about people who work for themselves, we have Amanda Turner. Good morning, Amanda. Tell us what you do.

Amanda: Well, basically I'm a cook. Unlike most cooks, who work at home or in a restaurant, I'm employed by various recording studios. When musicians are making an album, they have to stay in the studio all day, so I go there and prepare meals for them.

Presenter: Are musicians hard to please?

Amanda: Fortunately, they seem to be satisfied with what I do. When they're recording, they want something tasty but quite simple. They don't want to eat a lot, or be given unfamiliar dishes. The food has to be good for them because they're always worried about getting ill, or putting on weight.

Presenter: Would you call it a stressful job?

Amanda: It isn't usually. I only get worried when they forget to tell me how many people will want to eat, or when they tell me to expect five for a meal and then fifteen hungry people arrive! Often I don't have a proper kitchen to work in, and sometimes the meal is ready long before the musicians have finished playing. But I don't mind that.

Presenter: You're happy in your work then?

Amanda: Oh, yes. I know I'm lucky to do what I enjoy, and to get paid well for it. And I meet all sorts of interesting people! Think of your favourite boy band, and I've probably cooked them a meal! But I work with all kinds of musicians, pop and classical, famous and unknown, young and old. I'm happiest when I'm cooking for the young ones. They always *really* enjoy my food and say nice things about it.

Presenter: So how long is a typical day?

Amanda: *Very* long! I walk round the market early in the morning, buying vegetables and fresh meat and fish. I have to be at the studios by noon. I don't drive, and anyway it's always difficult to park, so they send a car to pick me up. Going on the bus with all my bags of shopping would be terrible! After cooking, serving and clearing up, I never get home before nine in the evening. My daughter prepares a snack for us while I tell her about the day's music. I also do a cookery page for a monthly magazine, so before I go to bed, I do some work on that. I always sleep really well!

Presenter: It sounds like a busy life! Thanks for talking to us, Amanda.

4　Writing

In PET Writing Part 3, students may write a story. They will either be given the title for a story or, as here, the first sentence.

Even if you ask students to write this story for homework, it will help if you let them prepare their stories in class first. Answering the questions given here, in pairs or small groups, will stimulate their ideas. Once the stories have been written, encourage students to check and improve them. They should see if they can make any points clearer by, for example, adding linking words. They should also see if they can avoid repeating words, or if they can add any interesting work-related words which they have learnt in this lesson. Ensure that they check for any grammatical errors (especially in verb tenses), and for any errors in spelling and punctuation.

4.1 House and home

Topic

The topic of this lesson is the home. PET reading and listening texts are often about everyday events in the home, and so are the pictures in PET Speaking Part 3. Students should be prepared to talk about the layout and furnishings of their own homes, and particularly their own rooms.

Lesson focus

The focus of this lesson is PET Listening Part 1, and most time should be spent on this activity.

1　Vocabulary

1 The first task introduces essential vocabulary for talking about the home. It can be done in pairs, small groups, or as a whole class activity. This is a good opportunity to discuss the layout of English houses and how it differs from those in the students' home countries. Discuss also the reasons for naming rooms, and their functions.

2 The second activity focuses on the type of furniture found in each room. Get students to divide the words in the box into four categories and then compare ideas. Rather than pre-teaching the vocabulary in the box, ask students to make use of picture dictionaries. Additional items of furniture, fixtures and fittings can then be added to the lists as an extra task.

Compare the English way of naming and positioning items with practices in the students' home countries. Remind them that some of the items might be found in more than one room.

KEY	
Living room:	coffee table, armchair, television, lamp, sofa
Kitchen:	dishwasher, sink, fridge, cooker
Bathroom:	washbasin, shower, towel rail, mirror
Bedroom:	wardrobe, chest of drawers, dressing table, television, lamp, mirror

2 Speaking

1 This activity is designed to help students deal with unknown vocabulary, especially in Part 3 of the Speaking paper, where they have to talk about a photograph. Students should try to describe or paraphrase words which they are unsure of in English.

Go through the example, explaining that a paraphrase usually includes both a description of the object and some explanation of what it is used for. Focus on the language used and ask students to talk about the objects in the list, using similar language.

2 The students are now ready to talk about the photographs. The locational language in the box is useful for the listening tasks which follow, and should be pre-taught thoroughly. Allow the students to discuss the photographs in pairs first, and then to report back about their ideas. Do not spend too long on this task, though; PET Speaking Part 3 is the focus of **Unit 6 Lesson 2**, and there is further practice in talking about photographs later in the book.

3 Listening 1.12

1 The listening provides a model of how to describe a room in a house. It is presented in the format of a PET Listening Part 1 task. For the moment, focus on the description and vocabulary. Allow students to listen and answer the question. Stop the CD and play the track again, if necessary.

KEY
C

RECORDING SCRIPT
In my room, there's not much furniture. I've got a bed, of course, but I don't have a wardrobe because I keep all my clothes in a chest of drawers. My parents don't like me putting posters on the wall, and for a long time I didn't have any, but I've recently been allowed to put up one or two. My parents bought me a desk to do my homework on, but I don't use it much. I like my room. It's nice.

2 This consolidates the vocabulary and topic of the lesson so far. It also provides some preliminary practice for PET Speaking Part 4. For now, focus on vocabulary and locational language. To encourage fluent speech, avoid monitoring language errors during the task.

4 Writing

Students can now consolidate the language they have learnt so far in this lesson by describing their own rooms. Remind them they must address all three bullet points in their answer and write no more than 45 words.

5 Listening 1.13–16

This exercise prepares students for PET Listening Part 1. In it, they hear a series of short texts and need to choose the visual related to the text, from a choice of three. Each recording is heard twice.

Texts may be either monologues or dialogues and are very short, usually consisting of no more than a few sentences or a couple of exchanges between speakers. Each text is independent of the others. No information is given about the text before students hear it, apart from the question. They should read each question carefully, and look at the pictures related to it, in the pause between the questions.

Students do not need to understand every word in the text, but should concentrate on finding the information necessary to answer the question. Generally speaking, all the information in the pictures is mentioned somewhere in the text, but only one picture is absolutely correct and answers the question. Students are not penalized for a wrong answer and should be prepared to make a guess at an answer if they are unsure.

Once you have introduced the aims of the listening task, go through the points in the **Get ready** box.

Play the first listening text and ask students to justify their choice of answer. Explain why the other answers are wrong. Then play the listening texts in **exercises 5.2–5.4**, stopping after each one and discussing the answers.

KEY
1 C   2 B   3 C   4 C

RECORDING SCRIPT
1
Boy: Mum, I can't find my mobile phone. It isn't on my bedside table.
Mum: Well, I haven't touched it. You sometimes put it in your drawer or perhaps it's still in the pocket of the jacket you were wearing last night. It's hanging up by the door.
Boy: No, I used it after I came in, and I was in my bedroom.

Mum: Well, you obviously still had your jacket on because it's in the pocket like I said.

Boy: Oh right.

2

And now a change to our schedule for this afternoon. The film, *Man of Destiny*, will not now begin at 3.45 as advertised. This is because there will be an extended edition of the news to report on today's exciting events in the athletics championships. The film will now be shown at four thirty-five. You can, however, still see the weather forecast at the normal time of 3.35.

3

Man: Would you like to order, Madam? The soup of the day is mushroom, served with garlic bread.

Woman: Oh, it's too hot for soup, but I want more than a salad. What do you suggest?

Man: Well, the fish is very good – that comes with either chips or a salad.

Woman: I see. Perhaps I'll just have a salad after all – I had some lovely fish for lunch, so perhaps I don't need so much this evening actually.

4   **Woman:** Hello, I've come to cut Susie's hair for her.

Man: Oh yes, come in. She's expecting you.

Woman: I wasn't sure what to bring. I've brought some special shampoo she might like to try, it's very good, and I've got scissors and a comb. But if she wants her hair washed, I might need to borrow something to dry it with, because I'm thinking of blow-drying it.

Man: Oh, I'm afraid we haven't got a hairdryer, but I can give you a towel if you want.

Interesting people

Topic

The topic of this lesson is families and people. This is a common topic in PET reading and listening texts. Students should be prepared to write and speak about their own families and to describe people they know, both in PET Writing Part 3 and in the Speaking paper.

Lesson focus

The main focus of this lesson is how to do PET Reading Part 4, and most time should be spent on this activity. A secondary focus is the useful skill of describing people.

1   Vocabulary

The purpose of this activity is to revise and extend students' vocabulary when talking about people. It also gives practice in describing people in photographs. This skill is necessary for PET Speaking Part 3.

1   The opening questions are an introduction to the topic and a warm-up. Ask the students these questions and have a short discussion with them about family parties.

2   The vocabulary given in the box acts as a series of prompts to help students describe people in the photograph.

Students often don't know what is expected of them when they're asked to talk about a photograph. Tell them that, if there are people in the photo, they can give a description of each person, including their:

- age and appearance, eg *he's middle-aged/fair-haired*
- clothes, eg *she's in blue jeans*
- activity, eg *he's pointing*
- facial expression and/or probable feelings, eg *he looks tired*

3–5   The purpose of these exercises is to revise and extend students' vocabulary for describing character and appearance. In pairs or groups, students share their knowledge. They can use dictionaries to check their answers.

KEY		
3	attractive/ugly	careful/careless
	cheerful/miserable	confident/shy
	foolish/wise	hard-working/lazy
	strong/weak	
4	amusing/funny	anxious/worried
	blond/fair	boring/dull
	understanding/patient	honest/truthful
	slim/thin	
5	Answers will depend on the students.	

2 Writing

This gives practice in writing the type of short message found in PET Writing Part 2. Students could either write the message in pairs in class, or do it as a homework exercise. Encourage them to use some of the vocabulary from the previous activity in their descriptions of their cousin.

It's useful to get students into the habit of checking their own writing before they hand it in to you. They should check they have included the three points given in the instructions and should attempt to correct any grammar, spelling and punctuation mistakes by themselves first.

KEY

Students' messages won't be exactly like this one, but they should clearly communicate the three points given in the instructions.

Model message:
```
To:     Robin
From:   Steffi

Could you meet my cousin Sofia for me at
the station this afternoon at 4.30? I
can't go because I've got my driving test
then. She's my age and is tall with dark,
curly hair. Thanks a lot.

Steffi
```

3 Reading

This prepares students for PET Reading Part 4. The reading text in this part of the paper is not long, but it has to be read very carefully. Students have to understand not only the factual details in the text, but also the writer's purpose. The student must also understand the writer's attitude or opinion, and the overall (global) meaning of the text. Students don't need to fully understand what is meant by 'writer purpose' or 'global meaning', as long as they are aware that these multiple-choice questions are slightly different from the ones they are familiar with.

1 Prepare students for the reading by asking them the introductory questions printed before the text. Encourage them to look at the photo of Shaun. Ask students to read the text carefully but, for the moment, to ignore any difficult words. Then ask them to answer the multiple-choice questions. They will probably find the questions quite difficult at this stage, so let them help each other by discussing the answers in pairs.

KEY

1 D   2 C   3 A   4 B   5 C

When discussing students' answers, refer to the **Get ready** box. Check students' answers to question 1, and then look at the first point in the **Get ready** box.

Now check students' answers to questions 2 and 3. These are testing details, and students should say which parts of the text give them the answers (paragraph 1, sentence 6 and paragraph 2, sentence 3).

Before checking students' answers to question 4, look at point 2 in the **Get ready** box. Although the focus here is on opinion rather than fact, students should be able to pick out the relevant parts of the text. (Shaun's attitude to studying: *'I love learning.'* Dr Wood's opinion: sentence beginning *'I don't care...'* Mrs Rogers' opinion: last two sentences of the text.) Then check students' answers to question 4.

Before checking students' answers to question 5, look at point 3 in the **Get ready** box. Students should underline the references to Shaun's age in the first paragraph, and *children who learnt at Shaun's speed* in the second paragraph. Students have to look at the whole text to find the correct answer to this question. They should eliminate **A**, **B** and **D** because *not all* the information in these sentences is correct according to the text. Check that students have chosen **C** as the correct answer.

Now answer any of the students' remaining queries on the text.

2 This task gives students more practice in understanding writer purpose. It gives a selection of possible writer purposes together with the vocabulary which describes these purposes (*recommend, compare*, etc). Ask students to match the purposes with the sentences. The purposes given here and in question 1 are all common purposes. Some other common purposes are: *show, say, tell, describe, report, give information about*.

Ready for PET

KEY
1 C 2 E 3 B 4 D 5 A

4 Writing

Students should be familiar with this type of sentence transformation exercise by now. Remind them they may have to use one, two or three words (never more) to complete the sentence. The sentences illustrate a variety of transformations found in PET Writing Part 1.

KEY
1 who is
2 strong enough
3 many students have
4 more/better than
5 (the) best/(the) most

5.1 Places of interest

Topic

The topic of this lesson is places and buildings. This is a common topic in PET, where the focus is often on places to visit and free-time activities. Students should be prepared to talk and write about places of interest they have visited. They should also be prepared to deal with the factual information that a potential visitor might need, in both written and spoken forms (brochures, guides, recorded information lines, etc.).

Lesson focus

The main focus of this lesson is how to approach PET Listening Part 3, and most time should be spent on this activity. A secondary focus is reading for information about places.

1 Reading

1   The purpose of this activity is to get students used to reading real-life visual information, such as notices, and to encourage them to name places where each might be found. Some of the words in the notices are above PET level, but each one contains a key piece of PET-level vocabulary that acts as the main clue. As this is a matching exercise, students should be able to guess if they're not sure.

Ask students to do the task in pairs. Elicit their answers and ask how they arrived at their choice.

KEY		
1 post office	2 sports centre	3 hotel
4 giftshop	5 post office	6 museum
7 sports centre	8 giftshop	9 hotel
10 museum		

2   Now ask the students to think about the type of information in the notices, and to divide them into three groups: a) giving information about what facilities are available; b) telling you what you must or mustn't do; and c) giving you simple information, for example *where* or *when*. This will help students to consider the message of each notice, as well as the words it uses.

KEY				
1 c)	2 c)	3 b)	4 a)	5 b)
6 b)	7 a)	8 b)	9 a)	10 a)

3 Ask students to think about other notices in similar places and how these might be expressed in English. Ask them to think of notices belonging to groups a), b) and c) for each of the places mentioned.

KEY

Example answers:

School:
a) Packed lunches are now available from the canteen.
b) Shoes must not be worn in the hall.
c) The school bus leaves from the main entrance.

Department store:
a) The coffee shop is open on the fifth floor.
b) This lift holds up to five people.
c) Sale begins Friday January 4th.

Bank:
a) New Savings Account 5% per annum.
b) Please wait here until a cashier is free.
c) This branch is open on Saturdays 10.00–13.00.

Airport:
a) Zone A: Check-in for domestic flights.
b) Please keep your baggage with you at all times.
c) BA 244 London: Please go to gate 16.

2 Listening 1.17–18

1–2 This section prepares students for PET Listening Part 3. Part 3 is a monologue lasting two or three minutes. Some of the information in the spoken text is also printed on the page, but there are gaps in this information which students are asked to fill in after listening.

The text may contain some words that are beyond the level of PET candidates, but these will be related to the context and will not be tested. Students should read the information on the page carefully during the pause between the end of Part 2 and the beginning of Part 3. This will prepare them to listen out for the information they need to complete the questions.

There is no fixed format to the questions, which may be in the form of a set of notes or sentences, presented as a notepad or other authentic frame. The two tasks in this section show two different layouts that may be found in Part 3 tasks. In each case, however, the answers required are short, generally a single word or number, or a very short phrase. If students think the answer is long and complicated, then they probably have the wrong answer!

Discourage students from writing down everything they hear in the hope of somehow including the right answer. They will almost certainly get no marks if they do this, as their answer will not make sense. Most answers will be nouns such as names or numbers, sometimes with adjectives of size, colour, etc.

Also explain to students that the words they need to write down will be clearly stated on the Audio CD, and will not need to be changed to form an answer. However, this is not a dictation exercise. Students should not expect the words they hear to match the words on the question paper exactly. They need to listen to extract the appropriate piece of information.

Read the **Get ready** box with the students and work through the two listenings. Remind them that in the exam there is only one text and a task with six questions.

Give students time to read the written information before the first listening, and play each listening text twice, as in the exam. During the first listening, they should follow the text on the page and write down any answers they are sure of. They should also be able to locate the other answers even if they didn't catch the key word or phrase. During the second listening, they can check what they have already written and locate any information that is still missing.

Encourage students to check their spelling at this stage, as a misspelling could create a word with a different meaning, eg *ship/sheep*. Students are not penalized for misspellings, but they could lose marks if their answer is not obviously correct.

KEY

1
1 one (1) hour
2 (your own / a) car
3 monkey
4 (a) picnic(s)
5 October
6 gift shop

2
1 one thousand (1,000)
2 prison
3 hotel
4 art gallery
5 theatre
6 0871 873 1256

Ready for PET

RECORDING SCRIPT

1 An interesting place to visit while you're staying in England is Woburn Safari Park. This is a place where you can see exciting wild animals from all over the world, but it's not a zoo because the animals do not live in cages. The animals are actually living in a large piece of English countryside, only an hour away from the centre of London, and about the same distance from the country's second city, Birmingham.

Woburn Safari Park is a great place to go for a day out because you can see lots of exciting animals as you drive round the park. And you're not taken round in a coach, you can actually take your own car around a special route that takes you to the parts of the park where the animals live.

And there are animals there from all over the world, including lions and tigers, four completely different sorts of monkey and things like giraffes and elephants too.

There are some rules, of course, both for your own safety and to protect the animals. You can't walk around the park, for instance, and you have to keep your doors and windows closed at all times. Oh, and you're not permitted to eat picnics in the area where the animals live.

So if you're interested in visiting the park, it opens at Easter each year, usually around the beginning of April and you can visit until the 30th October. August is the busiest time, of course, and you might see more people than animals if you go then, but May or September are good months to visit the park.

And when you've completed your tour of the Safari Park, there are other things to do at Woburn. For young people, there is a children's playground and an education centre which has information about the animals. And everyone will enjoy visiting the gift shop where you can buy all sorts of interesting souvenirs of your visit. For more information about …

2 Now there are lots of things to see and do in the university city of Oxford, especially the old college buildings and the walks along the river. But if you've done all that, and you're looking for a new experience, why not try Oxford Castle?

There's been a castle there for about one thousand years, although the buildings you see today are not as old as that, they're mostly around three hundred years old. In fact, for many years, the present castle buildings were not used as a castle at all. This is because what was called Oxford Castle was actually used as the city's prison. The castle is right in the centre of Oxford, which attracts many tourists from all over the world each year and now the old castle buildings have found a new use.

The buildings are now modernised and most of them are now part of a large hotel. There are 94 bedrooms and a good restaurant, but this is not the main attraction for tourists at the castle. Most of them will want to visit the museum which is in one of the oldest buildings and there is also an art gallery where you can see work by local artists.

In the summer, there is also a lot to do outdoors at the castle. During the day, there is a craft market where you can buy lots of local products, and in the evening there is an open-air theatre. There are also some very nice cafés and shops in the streets near the castle, which you'll enjoy looking round after your visit.

So if you'd like more information about Oxford Castle, this is the number to ring: 0871 873 1256 or log on to the website www.oxfordcastle.com. Next on the programme …

3 Reading

PET Reading Part 3 presents students with correct/incorrect questions about a text. Students have already practised this type of task in **Unit 3 Lesson 1**. Remind them of any points raised in that section before they do this task.

KEY

1 Incorrect	2 Incorrect	3 Correct	4 Correct
5 Incorrect	6 Correct	7 Correct	8 Correct
9 Incorrect			

4 Speaking

1 Students can now consolidate what they have learnt in the reading task by relating newly acquired words to their own country or locality.

2 This task is similar to that in PET Speaking Part 4. It gives fluency practice and consolidation; monitor for errors in language only.

5.2 Getting there

Topic

The topic of this lesson is transport and related services. Ideas connected with these everyday subjects may come up in any part of PET. Students should be prepared to write and speak about their own experiences using public and private transport. They should also be able to describe what transport is like in their country, and in places they have visited.

Lesson focus

The focus of this lesson is preparation for PET Reading Part 1, and most time should be spent on this activity.

1 Vocabulary

1 The purpose of this task is to activate and extend vocabulary related to transport. In the box there is a mixture of nouns, verbs and phrasal verbs to put under four headings. Although students are not expected to know many phrasal verbs at PET level, some commonly used ones will be very useful to them. Point out to students that some words fit into more than one category.

> **KEY**
>
> **Taxi:** driver, catch, fare, take, meter
>
> **Train:** driver, catch, miss, get on, ticket, fare, station, take, platform, timetable
>
> **Bus/coach:** driver, catch, miss, get on, ticket, fare, station, take, timetable
>
> **Plane:** pilot, attendant, land, catch, miss, get on, take off, check in, ticket, fare, gate, take, boarding pass, timetable

As you elicit the answers, encourage students to complete the table with all the words and to use it as a source of reference for their written work and when they are revising.

This is a good opportunity to discuss the conventions of travel in different parts of the world and make sure that those without experience of all the means of transport in the task (eg flying, long-distance train travel) understand what is involved.

2 The second task gives students the chance to select the right word in context.

> **KEY**
>
> 1 miss, station
> 2 catch/take, fare, tickets
> 3 check in, boarding pass, gate, get on
> 4 platform, ticket, get on
> 5 timetable, catch

2 Speaking

The purpose of this task is to encourage students to look at a photograph in detail and comment on those details. This skill is useful for any descriptive task involving photographs. It also elicits some further vocabulary related to transport.

Some vocabulary may need to be pre-taught.

Allow the students to do the task in pairs, for fluency practice; monitor for errors in vocabulary and structure only. Elicit the students' ideas and have a class discussion about transport and travel in general, and flying in particular. This could include their experiences, how transport is changing, what represents good service and value, etc.

3 Reading

1 In PET Reading Part 1 there are five very short texts which are either taken from a public notice, eg a sign or a label, or from a private note, eg an email or a postcard. Multiple-choice questions test the student's understanding of the message in each short text.

Students should read each notice very carefully and think about the place or situation in which they might expect to find it. They should also think about the purpose of the notice, what information it is conveying, and to whom.

> **KEY**
>
> A taxi   B train   C plane
> D bus/coach   E bus/coach

2 Go through the points in the **Get ready** box with the students. It is useful for students to think about the notices, signs, messages and labels they see in their daily lives, both in their own language and in English. As a warm-up exercise, you could give them some situations, for example: a library, a music CD cover, a zoo, their e-mail Inbox. Ask what notices, signs or messages they might expect to see there, and why.

Ready for PET

KEY
C

3 Work through the examples in **exercises 3.2** and **3.3**. In each case, give students the correct answer. Explain that the correct answer is the one that best matches the information or message in the notice.

KEY
1 C 2 C 3 C 4 A 5 C

4 Writing

Students can now consolidate the language they have learnt so far in this lesson by writing their own e-mail message. Remind them that they must address all three bullet points in their answer and write no more than 45 words.

6.1 What a bargain!

Topic

The topics of this lesson are clothes, shopping and money. Ideas connected with these everyday subjects may come up in any part of PET. Students should be prepared to write and speak about their own clothes preferences and shopping experiences.

Lesson focus

The focus of this lesson is how to do PET Writing Part 3, and most time should be spent on this activity.

1 Vocabulary

The purpose of this activity is to revise and extend students' clothes vocabulary. The vocabulary activated in trying to explain the differences between the words is just as important as the words in the box. Let students do the task first in pairs or groups. Monitor them, and don't let them simply take the easy way out by translating the words into their own language. Give help if necessary, and write any new words on the board. The differences may be explained in a variety of ways. Afterwards, discuss the differences between the words with the whole class.

2 Reading

This task gives students practice in the type of matching activity found in PET Reading Part 1. It can be done quite quickly.

KEY
1 D 2 A 3 C

3 Vocabulary

The purpose of this activity is to revise and extend students' money-related vocabulary. Point out that each missing word has the same number of letters as there are dashes. Do the first sentence as an example with the whole class and then ask them to complete the exercise in pairs or groups. Suggest that they first guess what each missing word is before searching for it in the word square. If they are having problems with any word, give them the first letter.

KEY	
1 earn, save	2 cheque, credit
3 note, coin	4 receipt, owe
5 lend	6 shop
7 charge	8 tip

4 Writing

1 In PET Writing Part 3, students are given a choice of topic. They may either write an informal letter or a story. The activities here prepare students for the letter-writing option. (There is practice in writing stories in **lessons 2.2, 3.2, 9.2** and **10.1**.)

Students are instructed to write their letter or story in about 100 words, and they shouldn't write many more than this. There isn't space to write much more than this on the answer sheet (see pages 88–89 of the Coursebook) and the more students write, the more mistakes they are likely to make! Students will not gain more marks for writing a longer answer. They won't be penalized if their answer is overlong (providing that the extra material is relevant to the topic). However, if they write fewer than 80 words they will lose marks.

The Writing Part 3 task carries a maximum of 15 marks. The focus of assessment in both the letter and story options is on the control and range of language used, and on the coherent organization of ideas. For more information about how PET Writing Part 3 is assessed, refer to pages 5–6 and 57–60.

In the letter-writing option, students are asked to write an informal letter, usually to an English-speaking friend. They are given some sort of stimulus (usually an extract from a letter from the English-speaking friend), which gives the topic for the letter that the students should write. The topic is usually quite broad, and will be related to daily life and other common areas of experience, for example, shopping, clothes, favourite television programmes, holidays, celebrations, school activities, free-time activities, etc. There may be some specific questions in the English-speaking friend's letter (eg '*Do you like shopping?*', '*Are there any good stores near you?*'), which students should answer, but they are free to develop the topic in the way that interests them. They should keep to the topic given for the whole letter, and not introduce unrelated ideas.

The task may involve describing people, feelings, likes and dislikes, habits, customs, past events or future plans. It may also require comparing different aspects of a topic (eg shopping for food and shopping for clothes) and giving an opinion. Students will be expected to demonstrate that they can organize their ideas clearly, attempt some complex sentence patterns (using, for example, time clauses, relative clauses, conditionals and comparatives, where appropriate), and employ simple linking words and phrases like *so, because, usually, best of all,* or *in fact*.

Students are **not** expected to include addresses in their letters, but they should use an appropriate layout. In other words, they should begin '*Dear* (name of friend),' and follow this with some kind of formulaic opening sentence (eg '*Thank you for your letter*'). They should also finish their letters with an appropriate concluding sentence (eg '*Please write to me again soon*'), a signing-off phrase (eg '*Love*') and a signature.

2 Do the gap-filling task quite quickly. Its purpose is to let the students become familiar with the content of the letter, and to make them look closely at the language. Once students have filled in the gaps, go through the answers with the class. Point out that once the gaps in Angela's letter to Chris have been correctly filled in, the letter serves as a 'model' of what is expected in this PET writing task.

The questions in this exercise have several uses. They show various ways to begin and end a letter, and the importance of identifying the required topic. They also suggest various strategies to help students develop their thoughts about the topic, such as:

- identifying different aspects of the topic (eg shopping for food, clothes and CDs), and the ideas related to each. Point out that Angela has written about the three different kinds of shopping in separate paragraphs;
- giving reasons (eg for liking or disliking something);
- giving examples (eg details of what happens on certain occasions).

Once you have gone through the answers with the class read through the points in the **Get ready** box.

KEY		
1 for	2 with	3 it/that
4 is	5 and/or	6 for
7 have	8 go	9 on
10 we	11 going	12 spend
13 the	14 a	15 me

Topic: shopping, in both letters
Different kinds of shopping: food, clothes, CDs
Angela's reasons for disliking food shopping are *The supermarket is always crowded* and *it's boring*.
Angela's examples of things she does when shopping are trying on clothes and not buying anything, and spending hours listening to the latest CDs.

> **Angela's 'hello' sentence:** *'Thank you for your letter.'*
> **Angela's 'goodbye' sentence:** *'Please write to me again soon.'*
> **Other 'hello' sentences:** *'I'm sorry I haven't written for a long time.' 'I was really pleased to hear your news.' 'It was great to hear from you again.'* The rest are 'goodbye' sentences.

3 This letter may be written in class or for homework. Students may develop their ideas on the topic in any way that interests them, as long as they don't wander from the topic of clothes (although they would be advised to say something about party clothes). Brainstorm the topic first in class, to help them develop some ideas. You could, for example, write the word CLOTHES in the middle of the board, and then surround it with other key words as you ask students (or they ask each other) questions about clothes, eg:

Do you wear the same clothes in summer and winter?
Do you wear the latest fashions?
How do you find out what they are?
Which clothes go out of fashion quickly?
Which clothes wear out quickly?
Which clothes have to last a long time?
What kind of clothes do you wear to school/parties/at home, etc?
What kind of clothes suits you best?
What kind of clothes do you feel most comfortable in?
What kind of clothes would you never wear?
Do you buy your clothes in department stores/boutiques/on the Internet, etc?
Can you make your own clothes?
Does/Did your mother make your clothes?
Do/Did you have to wear your older brother's/sister's old clothes?
Whose opinion about your clothes is most important to you?

Students should not attempt to write about *all* of these ideas. They should select a few of the ones they find interesting, and then organize them into paragraphs.

When they have written their letters, students should check that:

- they haven't strayed from the topic of clothes;
- they have organized their ideas clearly into paragraphs;
- they have written approximately 100 words;
- they have started with 'Dear ...' and written an appropriate 'hello' sentence;
- they have included a 'goodbye' sentence and a signature, with a signing-off phrase;
- they haven't only written simple sentences;
- they haven't made grammar or spelling mistakes;
- they have used commas and full stops where appropriate.

Use the PET markscheme on page 6 to give students marks for their letters.

5 Listening 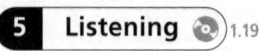 1.19

This activity gives students practice in the type of listening exercise found in PET Listening Part 3. Tell them to look at the advertisement before you play the recording, to get some idea of what they are going to hear and what they should listen out for. Remind them that they don't have to understand every word in the listening text to be able to write down the missing words correctly. Stop the CD after they've heard it once and play the track again. If students are still having trouble writing down any words, play the relevant sections of the recording again. Students should try to spell their answers correctly, although in this type of PET listening task any recognizable spelling is usually acceptable.

KEY

1 flowers **2** leather jackets **3** Sunday **4** a hospital

RECORDING SCRIPT

This is Radio London Fun calling all tourists in London! Did you know that East London has some of the most interesting street markets in Europe?

First up, there's Columbia Road market. You can buy flowers here at any one of 50 stalls. And whatever flowers you choose, they won't cost you much!

Next, there's Brick Lane market. Not everything here is new, but there's something for everybody. And if you're looking for a really good souvenir of London, then check out this market's speciality, leather jackets. You'll have to try one on!

Then, there's Petticoat Lane Market, the oldest and most famous of all London's markets. Buy anything here, from fashionable clothes to toys for the children. Come any morning from Monday to Friday, or on Sunday, when the market is at its biggest and most crowded.

Finally, there's Whitechapel market. It's easy to get to because it's right by the underground station, and just across the road from a hospital. This is the place to buy exotic vegetables and spices from Asia.

So, get down to East London now and be part of the fun!

6.2 City life

Topic

The topic of this lesson is various aspects of life in cities. Ideas connected with living in, or visiting cities may come up in most parts of the PET examination. Students should be prepared to write and speak about cities they know or have visited, and be prepared to describe how they feel about the way of life there.

Lesson focus

The focus of this lesson is PET Speaking Part 3, describing a photograph. Most time should be spent on this activity.

1 Vocabulary

1 This first task introduces the topic of city life through a pair of photographs. Students are encouraged to name as many things as possible in the photographs and then to focus on the activities taking place in them and the surrounding context. Students should work in pairs, with one student working on each photograph, as in the examination. In this task the focus is on vocabulary, so encourage students to help each other build up a list of vocabulary for each photograph. They shouldn't attempt to produce a full spoken description of the photographs at this stage.

2 Each student should now attempt to answer the questions about his or her own photograph. Students should take turns at answering each question with their partners.

3 Each student should take turns with his or her partner at comparing the photographs.

2 Speaking

1 This section develops the topic vocabulary further by asking students to compare city and country life. The first task is designed to help students develop fluency skills for Part 4 of the Speaking test, which will be the focus of the next lesson.

2 While they are doing this exercise, monitor the students. Give them feedback if necessary on the topic vocabulary, and help them with comparative structures to encourage fluency.

KEY

Answers will vary; some words can be used more than once.
a) **the city:** crowded, noisy, dirty, stressful, convenient, expensive, exciting, lonely, interesting, fun, dangerous, polluted.
b) **the country:** calm, peaceful, clean, boring, relaxing, safe, lonely, interesting, fun, inconvenient.

3 Students work in pairs to make lists. Monitor them and make suggestions, if necessary.

KEY

Some words can be used more than once.
a) **the city:** shopping, night-life, way of life, education, employment, transport, entertainment.
b) **the country:** fresh air, way of life, education, health.

4 This roleplay practises the language needed in PET Speaking Part 2. Revise some of the simpler language of agreement and disagreement before the students begin, and present the expressions given. Students work in pairs, as before. Encourage them to use the expressions given, and monitor them.

Before attempting the following activities, read through the **Get ready** box with the class. Explain that in Part 3 of the Speaking test, each student talks about one photograph. Although both photographs are based on the same theme, they have different contexts and vocabulary. This is the student's chance to produce a long turn (usually about 45 seconds to one minute) without interruption by the examiner or his or her partner. All that is expected at PET level, however, is a simple description of the photograph. This should be clear and comprehensible. It is an opportunity for students to show how good they are in their use of structures and vocabulary.

Make sure students understand the following:

- They should describe the photograph as if the examiner and their partner cannot see it. Nothing should be left out, even if it seems very obvious.
- There is no time limit; students do not have to speak for a whole minute.

- This is not a test of speed. Students should take their time and speak clearly.
- It is not necessary to name all the objects in the picture; students can use paraphrase, or simply say if they do not know a word.
- Marks are awarded for use of language, not for saying clever things.
- The task is simply to give a description, using a range of appropriate words and structures correctly.
- If students forget a word, or forget what they were going to say, they should just move on and talk about another part of the picture, not waste time trying to remember.
- There is no thinking or preparation time before the task begins.
- Time is short, so the student should keep talking to the examiner and their partner, make it interesting for them and try to speak clearly.

5 This task demonstrates how to approach the description of the photograph, how to find plenty of things to say about it, and how to structure things in a coherent way.

6–7 Students should work in pairs and take turns to talk about a photograph each. They should use the ideas in **5** to structure their descriptions. A description of the countryside photo may include these phrases:

'This photo was taken outside, somewhere in the countryside, probably in a garden...'

'There are four people. They are probably a mother and father with their two children. They look...'

'The family is having a meal. The boy is...'

Monitor the activity and give feedback after the students have finished.

The *Ready for PET* Audio CD includes a recording of students doing Practice Test 1, Paper 3 Speaking (pages 74–76 in the Coursebook). You can play it to your students as a model at this point. Refer also to page 53 of this book for more information about this sample Speaking test.

8 This task extends the topic of the lesson and involves discussions of the type found in PET Speaking Part 4. Monitor students for the correct use of the topic vocabulary only.

7 Food and drink

Topic

The topic of this lesson is food and drink. Ideas connected with eating and drinking may come up in any part of the PET examination. Students should be prepared to write and speak about their own food preferences. They should also be able to talk about various meals and places to eat, as well as local eating habits and customs.

Lesson focus

The focus of this lesson is PET Speaking Part 4, and most time should be spent on this activity.

1 Vocabulary

1 The purpose of this activity is to revise and extend students' food and drink vocabulary. If students are not familiar with many of the foods in the list, this can be turned into a dictionary exercise. Students can do the task in pairs or groups. When checking their answers, make sure they are aware of correct pronunciation, noting word stress in less familiar, longer words in particular.

KEY
Meat and fish: lamb, sausages, duck, beef, chicken, tuna, steak, burgers
Vegetables: carrots, beans, peas, onions, garlic, mushrooms, tomatoes, leeks, olives, spinach
Fruit: bananas, grapes, oranges, plums
Other: pasta, rice, mayonnaise, butter, cheese, pepper, salt, pizza

2 Students may like to add their favourite foods to the lists, especially those they may wish to talk about in the examination. Warn them not to talk about dishes and specialities which have no name in English, however, as these are usually very difficult to describe at this level.

2 Speaking

1 This activity builds on work done in **Unit 6 Lesson 2**. Remind students of the main points to consider when talking about a photograph, and let them work in pairs. Monitor vocabulary and speaking strategies.

2 This task gives fluency practice and allows students to personalize the subject matter.

Go through the **Get ready** box, which is designed to prepare students for PET Speaking Part 4. Part 4 is the freest part of the Speaking test. The examiner sets up an activity and leaves the students to complete it without any visual prompts. Each Part 4 task has two elements, eg *Talk about where you like to go and what you like to do there*. Students should listen carefully and try to cover both points in the discussion. Students get marks for the language they use, not for the content of what they say.

3 1.20 Let the students look again at the photographs on pages 42–43 of the Coursebook. Then play the examiner's instructions on the Audio CD to them. With the whole class, list possible things to talk about and questions to ask a partner. Ask the class for ideas on how to begin the conversation and write them on the board. In pairs, students attempt the conversation, using the expressions and subjects on the board. Monitor them, and give help if necessary.

KEY

The topic of the conversation is food that you eat when you go out and when you stay at home.

RECORDING SCRIPT

Examiner: Your photographs showed people eating a meal. Now I'd like you to talk together about the type of food you eat when you go out and when you stay at home.

4 1.21 Now play the conversation on the Audio CD to the students. (Point out that they will hear the examiner repeating the instructions given in **exercise 2.3** first.) Focus on how to begin, how to show interest, and how to manage turns. Discuss these points with the class, and write relevant expressions on the board.

RECORDING SCRIPT

Examiner: Your photographs showed people eating a meal. Now I'd like you to talk together about the type of food you eat when you go out and when you stay at home.

Girl: So, Tom, do you often eat out?

Tom: Sometimes... sometimes I go out for a meal with my family, and sometimes I go with my friends. What about you?

Girl: Yes, me too. What type of restaurant does your family go to?

Tom: Different types, but usually traditional ones. They like to have steak and chips and things like that, but I prefer Italian food...

Girl: Really! So do I. It's much more interesting than English food, isn't it?

Tom: Yes, I agree with you about that, and another thing is that it isn't very expensive.

Girl: That's right. When I go out with my friends, I always go to either an Italian or a Chinese restaurant.

Tom: Yes, me too... and also Thai... have you tried Thai food?

Girl: No, what's it like?

Tom: Well, it's similar to Chinese, but it has different tastes and unusual vegetables.

Girl: Oh, that sounds good!

Tom: Yes, you should try it.

5 In pairs, students should attempt a conversation about good restaurants and the food they like to eat in them. Encourage them to use the expressions from the Coursebook and those on the board. Monitor how they begin, show interest, and take turns. This part of the test requires students to talk fluently and spontaneously, in as natural a manner as possible. They need to build up confidence in their speaking, so ignore any language errors for now.

Ready for PET

3 Vocabulary

This activity deals with food preparation. It introduces language which is useful for students who want to describe their favourite dish, or another type of food, to someone less familiar with it.

1 1.22 Students should look at the visual material in pairs and complete the gaps in the list of ingredients. They can then discuss their ideas with the class. Afterwards, they listen to the Audio CD to check their ideas.

KEY

some **different-sized** tomatoes
a **small tin of** tuna fish
two spoonfuls of mayonnaise
a **hard-boiled** egg
some **black** olives
two spoonfuls of tomato sauce

You need: a mixing bowl, a fork and spoon, and a fairly sharp knife.

RECORDING SCRIPT

I'm going to tell you how to make tomato owls. First of all, you need some different-sized tomatoes, some big ones and some smaller ones, and a small tin of tuna fish. As well as these two main ingredients, you also need two spoonfuls of mayonnaise, a hard-boiled egg, and some black olives. To give colour, you will also need two spoonfuls of tomato sauce.

You don't have to cook the owls, but to make them you do need some basic equipment. Firstly, you need a mixing bowl to make the mixture in. To make the mixture you need a fork and a spoon, and to cut up the tomatoes and olives you need a fairly sharp knife.

2 1.23 Before attempting the next part of the task, pre-teach the verbs in the box. Ask any students who know the words to mime the action for the others in the class. Ask the students to complete the recipe in pairs; they then listen to the Audio CD to check their ideas. Play the Audio CD again so that they can complete the table. Do the first one with them as an example.

KEY

	Equipment	Verb	Ingredients
1	knife	cut	tomatoes
2	spoon	take out	seeds
3	mixing bowl	put in	tuna and egg
4	fork	mix	tuna and egg
5	spoon	stir in	mayonnaise and tomato sauce
6	spoon	put	mixture into tomatoes
7	knife	cut up	tomatoes and olives

RECORDING SCRIPT

So, now I'm going to tell you how to make the tomato owls. Firstly, take the knife and cut the tomatoes in half. Then take the spoon and use it to take the seeds out of the middle of the tomatoes, so that there's a hole for the mixture to go in. Then put the tuna and the hard-boiled egg into the mixing bowl. Then, using a fork, mix them together. When you have a good mixture, stir in the mayonnaise and the tomato sauce, using a spoon. Now take some of the mixture on the spoon and put it into the bottom half of each tomato. Cut the remaining tomato pieces into triangles to make the owl's mouth and ears, and cut up an olive to make its eyes.

4 Writing

This task practises the type of sentence transformation found in PET Writing Part 1. Students should already know how active and passive sentences are formed, but will probably need some revision. In PET, students are usually only asked to complete the active, rather than the passive sentence.

At this level, students also need to be familiar with simple reported speech and may, for example, be asked to complete a phrase in direct speech where the prompt is in reported speech. Students must therefore think about changes to the personal pronoun, the verb form, and the word order (for reported questions and requests).

KEY

1 usually prepares
2 finished all the
3 me not to
4 I have
5 order

7.2 Your own space

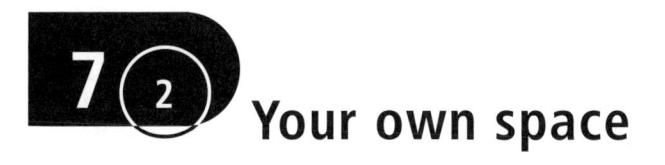

Topic

The topic of this lesson is personal space and getting on with other people. Living with your family is a common topic in the PET examination.

Lesson focus

The focus of this lesson is PET Listening Part 4, and most time should be spent on this activity.

1 Speaking

This activity is a lead-in to the topic of personal space. It also gives students practice in talking about their opinions and attitudes, building on the previous lesson.

First divide the class into pairs; students in each pair take turns at asking and answering the questions. Monitor them to see where gaps in vocabulary might be causing problems.

2 Reading

1 First ask students to read and complete the multiple-choice cloze exercise, which practises PET Reading Part 5. If they are unsure how to approach the task, do the first gap with them, explaining which option in the key is correct, and why.

KEY
1 B 2 C 3 B 4 C 5 B
6 D 7 A 8 D 9 B 10 C

2 The second task practises the type of multiple-choice questions found in PET Reading Part 4. If necessary, remind students of the points in **Unit 4 Lesson 2**, which deals with this part of the test. If you feel students need more structured fluency practice at this stage, ask them to work through the questions in pairs. Then go through the answers with the class.

KEY
1 C 2 B 3 B

3 Listening 1.24

Read through the **Get ready** box with the students and remind them that in this type of listening task they will need to:

- distinguish between male and female voices and names. The identity and gender of speakers is clearly indicated in spoken and written rubrics.
- listen for phrases of agreement and disagreement.
- listen for intonation, which relates to meaning.
- remember that the sentences on the question paper may refer to the past, present or future. Sentences do not usually repeat the words given on the Audio CD, but they may summarize the opinions of the speakers.
- give an answer. Wrong answers are not penalized, so it is worth giving any answer rather than none, even if they are not sure.

1 Make sure that students read the instructions before you play the Audio CD, and be prepared to answer any questions. Check that they know what to do.

2 The Audio CD should be played twice. Elicit students' answers and be ready to play sections of the Audio CD again, or provide a copy of the Recording Script.

KEY
1 A 2 B 3 B 4 A 5 A 6 B

RECORDING SCRIPT

Bob: Hello, Mary, how are you?

Mary: Oh, hello Bob. Not too bad. We're having one or two problems with our son, Matthew.

Bob: Really? What sort of problems?

Mary: Well, he wants to have his own bedroom, but we haven't got the space and he doesn't seem to understand.

Bob: Oh, so he shares with his brother, does he?

Mary: Yes, but there's not a great age difference, just one year, so you'd think they'd be able to get on together, wouldn't you?

Ready for PET

Bob: I remember I used to hate sharing a bedroom with my older brother. We used to argue all the time. Mostly about privacy, as I remember.

Mary: Privacy? You mean you wanted more time to be alone?

Bob: It wasn't that. It was more that I wanted to have my own space. You know, we had one wardrobe, one chest of drawers. I didn't even have one drawer that was all mine, and so my elder brother used to just take all my things if he fancied them.

Mary: Oh, I see. I wonder if that's Matthew's problem? Because he wanted his own computer, but there's not room for two in the one small bedroom, so we said no, they'd have to share.

Bob: So who gets to use it all the time?

Mary: I don't know, but they always seem to be fighting about something, and of course Matthew doesn't have as much homework as his brother, so maybe he doesn't need it so much.

Bob: Well, they're not only for doing homework on, you know.

Mary: I know that Bob, and they've got their own television in the room, but Matthew doesn't really seem to like television very much. I don't understand him sometimes.

Bob: Well, maybe it's because he doesn't get to watch the programmes he likes.

Mary: Actually, I think he'd rather not have the television in the room. I think I'd better talk to them about these things. Maybe we can arrange things better. Thanks Bob.

Bob: Don't mention it.

4 Speaking

Read the questions with the students and check that they understand them first. Let them answer the questions in pairs. Monitor and give help where necessary. Make sure that the students take turns at asking and answering with their partners. Encourage them to ask each other further questions, to develop a conversation.

5 Listening 1.25

First explain to the students that they are going to hear two teenagers, Alice and Harry, having a conversation. Give them time to read through the task and the sentences. Play the Audio CD once and let them tick their answers. Then play the Audio CD a second time so that they can check them and listen out for any missing information. Once this has been done, go through and elicit their answers and their reasons. Be prepared to replay sections of the Audio CD, or provide a copy of the Recording Script to answer any uncertainties.

KEY
1 A   2 B   3 A   4 A   5 B   6 B

RECORDING SCRIPT

Alice: Oh, hello Harry, how are you?

Harry: Fine, thanks. But you look a bit miserable. What's the matter?

Alice: I've been arguing with my mum again, I'm afraid. I feel sorry about it afterwards, but she just annoys me *so much*.

Harry: Yeah, I know what you mean. But what have you been arguing about?

Alice: Oh, the usual thing about my bedroom.

Harry: Your bedroom?

Alice: Yeah. She's always telling me to tidy it up, but it's my room, so I don't see why I should have to.

Harry: And is it really untidy, or is it just that she's *really* fussy about things like that?

Alice: Oh, it's untidy all right. I mean, you know, I take my clothes off at night and just leave them where they fall.

Harry: And you expect your mum to tidy up after you?

Alice: No, I do it sooner or later because it's not good for your stuff to be left screwed up in a ball, is it? It's just that she wants it done like *now*, and I'm happy to leave it for a while and do it later, you know, when I feel like it, or when I've got friends coming round.

Harry: And so you argue?

Alice: Yeah. She wants me to put everything back in the wardrobe, but I've got so much stuff that it won't all fit anyway.

Harry: You're lucky. I have to share a wardrobe with my brother. He's always wearing my things without asking me.

Alice: But don't you each have your own bedroom?

Harry: We do, but his is very small and you can't get a wardrobe in, so he's always coming in and out of my room to get stuff out of it.

Alice: Oh, I wouldn't like that.

Harry: Nor do I. It leads to *lots* of arguments.

6 Speaking

The photographs give students another opportunity to practise descriptions. Remind them of the strategies they used to describe a photograph in **Unit 6 Lesson 2**. Tell them to use paraphrase if they don't know a word.

Students should attempt the task in pairs. When they have finished, elicit any vocabulary problems and ask what paraphrase strategies they used to get round them.

8 1 Close to nature

Topic

The topics of this lesson are the natural environment, the weather and animals. Aspects of these topics may come up in any part of PET. Students should be prepared to write or speak about their opinions and experiences of them.

Lesson focus

The main focus of this lesson is how to do PET Reading Part 5, and most time should be spent on this activity. A secondary focus is Parts 2 and 4 of the PET Speaking paper.

1 Vocabulary

The purpose of this activity is to revise and extend the vocabulary students need to talk about the pollution of the environment. Aspects of this subject may come up in a PET reading text, and students should be familiar with the basic topic-related words. However, students are not expected to deal with complicated or technical aspects of the topic. They can do the activity in pairs or groups and share their knowledge.

KEY		
1 destroying	2 breathe	3 dusty
4 spoil	5 rubbish	6 minerals
7 fuels	8 poverty	9 prevent
10 rescue	11 urgent	12 inhabitants

2 Listening 1.26

1 The purpose of this activity is to give students practice for PET Listening Part 1 and also to revise and extend their weather-related vocabulary. To preview some of the vocabulary, ask students to describe the photos before they listen to the recording. Students should hear the recording twice before answering the question, so after the first listening stop the CD and play the track again.

KEY		
Speaker 1 B	Speaker 2 C	Speaker 3 A

RECORDING SCRIPT

1 I listened to the weather forecast before we set out and it wasn't encouraging – storms with thunder and lightning and even snow on the hills! Actually, it was a fine, clear day. There was frost on the ground when I woke up and some mist over the fields, but that soon disappeared in the warm sunshine. There were some clouds about, but the wind kept them moving and it didn't rain. All in all, it was a brilliant day!

2 It was lucky we didn't have far to walk on Saturday. I couldn't help slipping on the snow-covered pavements and the air was freezing! But, really, I like that kind of weather best. It kind of makes me feel alive - not like foggy days, or dull, damp ones when I just want to stay indoors, or very hot and sunny ones which send me to sleep! So it was a great day!

3 You know what they say about the weather being changeable? Well, it wasn't like that on Saturday! It was one heavy shower after another. Just when we thought it was going to dry up, it started pouring again! Still, it was quite warm, though it got cooler in the evening, so we didn't really mind. I heard later there were gales on the coast, so we escaped them! In spite of the weather, we really enjoyed our day!

2 Stop the CD and play the track a third time, pausing frequently to allow students time to write.

KEY

Good weather: fine, clear, warm, sunshine, hot, sunny, dry up

Bad weather: storms, thunder, lightning, snow, frost, mist, clouds, wind, rain, snow-covered, freezing, foggy, dull, damp, changeable, shower, pouring, cooler, gales

Other weather words: forecast, slipping

3 Speaking

This practises the type of discussion found in PET Speaking Part 4. Students write questions for each point and ask and answer in pairs. Remind them that they will be doing the Speaking test in pairs.

4 Reading

This prepares students for PET Reading Part 5. They have to complete each gap by choosing one of four multiple-choice options. Take students through the **Get ready** box before or after the multiple-choice questions.

KEY

1 A 2 C 3 D 4 B 5 D
6 A 7 B 8 C 9 B 10 A

5 Listening 1.27

In this activity, students practise PET Listening Part 2. Give students a few moments to read through the questions.

Play the recording once. Check the students' answers and respond to any of their queries.

KEY

1 C 2 A 3 C 4 B 5 B 6 A

RECORDING SCRIPT

Interviewer: In the studio today, I have Henry Tweedy and his dog, Lady. Henry, Lady is very special to you, isn't she?

Henry: Oh yes. We've only been together for six months but I couldn't do without her. I started going deaf when I was twenty and now I can't hear much at all. I can only understand you if I can see your mouth. Lady lets me know when the door bell rings, or my son cries, or about any important noise, at home or when we're out for walks. Guide dogs for the blind are common, but now dogs are regularly trained to help other kinds of disabled people.

Interviewer: Can any dog be trained like Lady?

Henry: Many can, and some disabled people ask to have their family pet trained. It helps if the dog is young, but even older dogs like Lady here can learn to do quite difficult things. Her trainer says he knew she was right for the job when he saw how clever she was and how well she got on with people. I'm glad he picked her for me.

Interviewer: What happened during her training?

Henry: Well, she spent four months at the training centre, learning to follow instructions and to recognise different sounds. Then the trainer worked with her for two months in my house so she could learn about me and where I live – so that was a six-month training period. The trainer still visits to check everything's going well but we haven't had any problems.

Interviewer: So, say Lady hears the doorbell, how does she let you know?

Henry: Well, first she usually runs towards the sound to check it out and then she comes back to tell me about it. She does that by pushing her nose into some part of my body. For the doorbell, it's my left knee.

Interviewer: And how do you tell her what to do?

Henry: She's always looking at me, ready for any command, and I talk to her with my hands – it's a kind of sign language. I sometimes reward her afterwards with a biscuit, but not all the time because it's bad for her.

Interviewer: Do you think Lady enjoys her work?

Henry: Oh, without a doubt! Dogs like having a job to do – they have quite a professional attitude to it! Lady is happiest when she's busy or learning to do something new. Many family dogs sleep most of the day but that's not really natural for them.

Interviewer: Well, thank you Henry, and Lady. It's been fascinating talking to you.

6 Speaking

This practises the type of activity found in PET Speaking Part 2. Students should do the activity in pairs and give reasons for their choices. Partners should react by agreeing, disagreeing, making an additional point, giving an example, etc. The discussion should also stimulate ideas for the writing task that follows.

7 Writing

This task prepares students for the letter-writing option in PET Writing Part 3. Students may write their letters in class or for homework. The English penfriend's letter, which is the stimulus for the task, invites the students to give their ideas, opinions and experiences of animals. They may develop the topic in any way that interests them, as long as they say something in response to the penfriend's question about pets and keep to the subject of animals. The previous reading, listening and speaking activities should have already stimulated a number of ideas about the topic.

Students could, for example, devote their whole letter to writing about their pet (where they got it, how they look after it, the games they play with it, how they feel about it). There are many other possibilities. One would be to write one paragraph about a visit to a zoo (watching animals in captivity), and contrast this with another paragraph about a visit to the countryside (watching animals in their natural environment).

Encourage students to check their own work before they hand it in to you.

8.2 The wide world

Topic

The topic of this lesson is geography and the world. Aspects of this topic may come up in any part of PET.

Lesson focus

The main focus of this lesson is how to do PET Writing Part 1, and most time should be spent on this activity. A secondary focus is practice for PET Speaking Part 2.

1 Reading

1 This activity practises the type of exercise found in PET Reading Part 3. It also revises some of the vocabulary needed to talk about different features of the countryside. The initial questions introduce the topic.

2 Let students read through the sentences and check that they understand them first. They then read through the text individually, deciding for themselves whether the sentences are correct or incorrect. After the students have completed the task and you have checked the answers with the class, ask them to underline words in the second and third paragraphs of the text which refer to different features of the countryside.

Ask them which of these words they could use when describing their own country. Then get them to suggest other words which describe different parts of their country and write them on the board.

KEY
1 incorrect 2 correct 3 incorrect 4 correct 5 correct

2 Vocabulary

The purpose of this activity is to revise and extend the vocabulary of geographical features. It builds on the vocabulary introduced in the text about Sri Lanka. Encourage students to share their knowledge. They can do the activity in pairs or groups. **Note:** Students may find alternative answers to the ones in the key. This is acceptable, provided they can justify their choices.

KEY

1 *desert* because it's not a word for a high place
2 *waterfall* because it's not an area of land
3 *island* because it isn't a place with a lot of trees
4 *cave* because it's not water
5 *bay* because it's not a kind of earth
6 *wave* because you can't walk down it
7 *valley* because it's not part of the coastline
8 *flood* because it isn't the limit of something

3 Speaking

This activity practises the type of task found in PET Speaking Part 2. The initial questions introduce the topic. The task gives students an opportunity to use some of the vocabulary from the previous two activities.

Make sure students understand the instructions before they look at the illustrations and discuss them in pairs. Students do this type of activity in pairs in the PET Speaking test. In their discussions, which should last for about three minutes, students should:

- imagine themselves in the situation
- say something about *each* picture (in this case, what adventures the hero and heroine could have in each place)
- come to a conclusion (in this case, which location will be the most exciting) only after each picture has been discussed
- give reasons for their choice
- interact with each other – that is, they should listen to what the other person says and then react to it. This will involve: giving an opinion; giving a reason for an opinion; asking a question; answering the partner's question; agreeing or disagreeing with what the partner has said (with a reason); making a further point; adding an example; introducing a new point (or going on to another picture); and so on.

After about three minutes, stop the discussion and review how the students dealt with the task.

- Find out whether they managed to say something about each illustration. Brainstorm possible 'adventures' for each picture. Supply any appropriate vocabulary that students need.
- On the board, build up a list of 'discussion' language, eg *I think X is more exciting because...*, *That's a good point*, etc. (See Unit 2, Lesson 1.)
- Ask students whether both partners contributed an equal amount to the discussion. Quieter students should make an effort to say more, and over-dominant students should try to include their partners more in the discussion. Being good at taking turns is something the examiners look for.

Students now find a different partner and attempt the task again. This time their performance should be better.

4 Writing

1   This activity prepares students for PET Writing Part 1. In this test task, they are given five sentences with a common theme. Students have to complete sentences which are similar in meaning, using a different structural pattern. They may have to use one, two or three words in their answer, but they should never use more than three words. Contractions count as two words. The task mainly focuses on knowledge of grammar, but some knowledge of vocabulary will also be required. Students must make sure that the completed second sentence has the same meaning as the first. There is one mark for each sentence in this part and the student's answer must be completely correct (including spelling) to gain the mark. Sometimes there may be more than one possible correct answer for each sentence.

By now, students should be familiar with this type of task. Ask them to complete the sentences about geography, and then take them through the points in the **Get ready** box. They may wish to correct their own work as they do this.

KEY

1 far from
2 (ever) going for
3 you look at
4 have been
5 you like to

2   Once you have checked all the answers to **exercise 4.1**, ask students to do the next five sentences. Check answers and deal with any queries that arise.

KEY

1 took
2 as/so heavy as
3 difficult for
4 find/have found
5 so has

5 Reading

This gives practice in understanding the type of short reading text which may be found in PET Reading Part 1. It can be done quite quickly.

KEY

1 A   2 C

9.1 Free time

Topic

The topic of this lesson is sport, hobbies and other leisure activities. Aspects of this topic may come up in any part of PET. Students should be prepared to write or speak about their own sporting and leisure interests.

Lesson focus

The focus of this lesson is a revision of exam skills for the PET Reading paper.

1 Vocabulary

1 The anagrams are a warm-up activity, so don't let students spend too much time on them. Give them the first letter of each word if they have difficulty completing the task.

KEY

1 windsurfing   2 table-tennis
3 golf   4 gymnastics
5 judo   6 hockey
7 baseball

2 The questions after the anagrams revise and extend the vocabulary needed to talk about sport.

Examples:
ball, bat, racket, net, goal, goal post, game, match, hit, kick, shoot, team, race, race track, sports field, stadium, speed, win, lose, score.

2 Reading

This gives students practice in the type of exercise found in PET Reading Part 2. If necessary, refer students back to the **Get ready** box in **Unit 2 Lesson 2**. If you think your students need extra practice doing test tasks within a time limit, tell them they only have ten minutes to complete the task.

KEY

1 F   2 A   3 D   4 G   5 C

Now go through the points in the **Get ready** box with the students, and discuss them. Refer back to other units, where necessary, to remind them about the different parts of the Reading paper. (For Part 1 – **Unit 5 Lesson 2**; for Part 2 – **Unit 2 Lesson 2**; for Part 3 – **Unit 3 Lesson 1**; for Part 4 – **Unit 4 Lesson 2**; and for Part 5 – **Unit 8 Lesson 1**.)

Tell them that they have already practised all the different types of reading tasks found in PET. Before they actually do the test, you should give students:

- a reminder of what to expect in the test (refer them to page 2 in the Coursebook)
- instructions on how to record their answers in the test (see the **Get ready** box)
- experience of doing a complete, timed practice paper.

Students need to practise doing a timed paper so that they can find out how much time to spend on each question. If they spend too much time on one part, they might not manage to finish the paper, or they might have to rush through the last questions. Equally, they shouldn't hurry to complete the paper in less than the time allowed. Each text and its questions needs to be approached carefully.

There are 35 possible marks for the Reading part of the test, one mark for each question. These 35 marks are then adjusted so that they represent 25% of the total marks available for the test.

Make sure students understand how they should record their answers. Refer them to the sample answer sheets on pages 88–89 of the Coursebook. These may be photocopied for use with a practice paper.

Reassure students that they don't have to understand every word in the reading texts to be able to answer the questions. By now, they should have got used to guessing the meaning of unknown words from their context, and feel confident enough with their reading skills to ignore unknown words in less important sections of text.

At some point soon, either now or when you have revised the content of the Writing paper in the next lesson, you should give the students a timed, complete Reading and Writing paper. Use the papers from one or both of the Practice Tests at the back of the Coursebook for this. Refer to page 4 for advice on the practice test.

You can use PET past papers, as well as the Practice Tests at the back of the Coursebook, with your students. Remember also that there are six practice tests on the *Ready for PET* CD-ROM.

Ready for PET

3 Vocabulary

1 The purpose of this exercise is to revise and extend the vocabulary students need to talk about free-time activities, and, in particular, their own hobbies and interests. Students should do the matching task in pairs or groups.

KEY

1 material, needle, scissors, pins, refreshing drink
2 brush, hammer, nails, paint, refreshing drink
3 dictionary, envelope, notepaper, stamp, refreshing drink
4 flower pot, watering can, seeds, spade, refreshing drink
5 balls, net, racket, sports bag, refreshing drink

2 Students go on to tell each other about their own free-time activities. This will activate vocabulary for the following PET Speaking Part 2 task.

4 Speaking

This practises the type of task found in PET Speaking Part 2. Students should do the activity in pairs. Before they start:

- make sure they understand what they are to do;
- point out to them that the discussion has a double focus (*how interesting the different hobbies are* and *which will be best for making friends*), and tell them that they should talk about both of these aspects;
- remind them that they need to to keep the discussion going for three minutes; that they should say something about each illustration; and that they should *interact* with their partner.

9.2 Get well soon!

Topic

The topic of this lesson is health and sickness. Aspects of this topic may come up in any part of PET. Students should be prepared to write and speak, in a simple way, about common illnesses and their own health and fitness lifestyles.

Lesson focus

The focus of this lesson is a revision of exam skills for the PET Writing paper.

1 Writing

This practises the type of task found in PET Writing Part 2.

1 The topic of health and fitness is introduced by the questions. Elicit the students' opinions and in the discussion, ask for their views on their sleeping habits, eating habits, exercise routines, and any unhealthy habits they may have (eg smoking). Also ask them about any activities they do to relax.

2 Before doing this task, refer students back to the **Get ready** box in **Unit 1 Lesson 2**. If you think your students need extra practice doing test tasks within a time limit, tell them they only have seven minutes to complete the task. Remind them to check their work.

KEY

Students' answers won't be exactly like this one, but they should cover the three points given in the instructions.

Model answer:
```
To:   Alex
From: Juan
From now on, I'm going to sleep 8
hours a night. I'm going to give up
chips and chocolate and eat more
fish, salad, fruit and vegetables.
Why don't we join a gym together and
go there every day after school?
Juan
```

2 Vocabulary

The purpose of this activity is to revise and extend the vocabulary needed to talk, at a simple level, about health and sickness. Point out to students that the number of dashes in the space in the sentence corresponds to the number of letters in the missing word. Do the first sentence as an example with the whole class, and then ask them to complete the exercise in pairs or groups. Suggest that they first guess what each missing word is before searching for it in the word square. Give them the first letter of problem words.

KEY

1 emergency, accident, ambulance
2 earache, clinic, pill, pain
3 deaf
4 nurse, patient
5 drug, fit
6 ill, sore, cough, flu
7 wound, pale, dizzy, faint

3 Reading

Before doing this task, refer students back to the **Get ready** box in **Unit 4 Lesson 2**. If you think your students need extra practice doing test tasks within a time limit, tell them they only have ten minutes to complete the task.

KEY

1 D 2 A 3 D 4 B 5 C

4 Writing

This practises the type of task found in PET Writing Part 1. Before they start, refer students back to the **Get ready** box in **Unit 8 Lesson 2**. If you think your students need extra practice doing test tasks within a time limit, tell them they only have five minutes to complete the task. The sentence patterns given here are frequently tested in PET.

KEY

1 my head was
2 keep fit
3 you give up
4 have (got)
5 can't/mustn't/shouldn't/may not smoke

5 Writing

This activity practises the type of task found in PET Writing Part 3. It may be done in class or for homework. Refer students back to the **Get ready** box in **Unit 6 Lesson 1** first. Advise them to think carefully about both writing tasks before deciding which one they can write best. Emphasize that they write *either* the letter *or* the story. If you think your students need extra practice doing test tasks within a time limit, tell them they only have 20 minutes to complete the task. Remind them to:

- write approximately 100 words;
- organize their ideas clearly into paragraphs;
- use a range of structures and vocabulary if possible, and write complex sentences where appropriate;
- use linking words where appropriate;
- check their work carefully.

Use the PET markscheme on page 6 to give students marks for their writing. Also refer to the **Examples of student writing** on pages 57–60.

Now go through the points in the **Get ready** box with the students. Reassure them that earlier in the book, and in this lesson, they have practised all the different types of writing tasks found in PET. Give students:

- a reminder of what to expect in the test (refer them to the chart on page 2 of the Coursebook);
- instructions on how to record their answers in the test (see the **Get ready** box);
- experience of doing a complete, timed practice paper.

Refer to page 4 for advice on how to administer a practice test.

Before students attempt a complete practice paper, ask them to estimate the amount of time they should spend on each part, bearing in mind that they should leave some time at the end to check their answers. After they have done a practice test, ask them whether their estimate was accurate. Did they, for example, spend an equal amount of time on each part of the Reading paper, or did some parts need more time than others? How about the amount of time they allowed for writing the letter – was it too much, too little, or just right? Thinking about this should help students to use their time efficiently in the real test.

10.1 Entertainment

Topic

The topic of this lesson is entertainment. Aspects of this topic may come up in any part of PET. Students should be prepared to write and speak about their own likes and dislikes in the area of entertainment and give reasons for their views.

Lesson focus

The focus of this lesson is a revision of the exam skills needed for the PET Listening paper.

1 Speaking

1 This task is an introduction to the topic and revises adverbs of frequency. Check that students understand both the meaning of the adverbs and how they are used in a sentence. The question 'How often... ?' is commonly used in PET. Make sure that students fully understand when and how it should be used.

2 The second task introduces vocabulary related to entertainment. Ask students to add some more words to the list for each activity, and encourage them to ask for more.

KEY

1 **curtain:** theatre, concert
2 **interval:** concert, theatre, cinema
3 **ticket:** cinema, concert, theatre, clubbing
4 **encore:** concert, theatre
5 **soap opera:** television
6 **channel:** television
7 **website:** the Internet
8 **programme:** television, concert, theatre
9 **soloist:** concert
10 **commercial:** television, cinema
11 **backing group:** concert
12 **chat room:** the Internet

3 This activates vocabulary related to entertainment. Let students work with a partner and monitor them.

2 Vocabulary

1 In this task, students must use the topic vocabulary in context. Encourage students to attempt the task first by using the words they know and guessing the others. Elicit answers and clarify meanings afterwards.

KEY

1 series	2 part	3 lines
4 rehearsal	5 stage	6 clap
7 reviews	8 studio	9 camera
10 director	11 performance	12 screen

2 Make sure that students reread the whole text before attempting the questions. They focus on understanding the actor's attitudes (*gist meaning*).

KEY

1 C   2 A

3 This exercise enables students to name a type of performer and explain what that person does.

KEY

1 journalist   2 plays

4 Now ask the students to write some more sentences based on this model.

3 Listening 1.28–30

1–2 The first two tasks practise listening to a recording and answering multiple-choice questions using pictures, as in PET Listening Part 1. Refer students back to **Unit 4 Lesson 1**.

KEY

1 B   2 C

3 The third task, a verbal multiple-choice, is found in PET Listening Part 2. More of these tasks are found in the Practice Listening Tests on pages 72–74 and 83–85 of the Coursebook.

KEY

A

RECORDING SCRIPT

1 Man: What do you feel like doing tonight? I'm getting a bit tired of clubbing.

Woman: Yeah, me too. How about going to the open-air concert? The guitarist is meant to be *really* good.

Man: Oh, I heard that all the tickets were sold out weeks ago, but there's a good film on at the ABC. You know, it's the one that won all the Oscars.

Woman: OK, and if we can't get in, there's always the theatre next door. That's never full, so it's a good idea.

2 Woman: It's *great*, this new cinema! *Four* films on at the same time, and they're all good.

Man: Well, I don't know about that. There's a good thriller on in Screen Number One, or I wouldn't mind seeing the science fiction one, that's meant to be really good.

Woman: Well, I'm not keen on seeing either of those. But how about the one about animals, that's much more my sort of thing than the other one… what is it? Some sort of romantic comedy?

Man: That's right. Oh well, I'm quite happy to go along with your choice.

3 Man: So, what did you think of it?

Woman: Well, he's a brilliant director, isn't he? All those lovely scenes in the mountains… the camerawork was *wonderful*.

Man: I thought the actors were good on the whole, although to be honest, I think the storyline, the plot, is *so* strong that you don't worry so much about the characters. I mean, it is a classic action film, isn't it?

Woman: I *absolutely* agree with you. I was on the edge of my seat the whole time! You never knew what was going to happen next. That's what *really* made it for me.

Man: Oh yeah, me too.

4 Speaking

This task activates vocabulary which has already been acquired. Pre-teach some additional vocabulary before the students begin.

Examples:
the star/the co-star   *the hero/the heroine*
funny/serious/sad   *entertaining/dull*
the beginning/the ending

Students prepare what they will say to their partners for a few minutes before they take turns at presenting their ideas. Monitor and give help if necessary.

5 Listening 1.31

Now go through the **Get ready** box with the students. Point out that they have already practised all the different types of listening task found in PET.

Refer students to the **Get ready** boxes in earlier units which focus on the various parts of the Listening test. (For Part 1 – **Unit 4 Lesson 1**; for Part 2 – **Unit 3 Lesson 2**; for Part 3 – **Unit 5 Lesson 1**; and for Part 4 – **Unit 7 Lesson 2**.) Students often feel most anxious about the Listening test and think they have done badly. Encourage students to feel confident about their ability to listen, to keep calm, and to answer all the questions as best they can.

Make sure that students understand how they should record their answers and when they should copy their answers onto the answer sheets. (They should be given six minutes at the end of each practice test to do this.) Refer them to the sample Answer Sheet on page 89 of the Coursebook.

Before they do the PET examination students need to do a complete paper under timed conditions so that they can get used to the answer sheets, and learn how to use their time efficiently. There are two Listening Tests on pages 72–74 and 83–85 of the Coursebook. At least one of these should be conducted under timed conditions. Advice on how to administer a practice test is given on page 4.

Note that in the PET Listening test, each listening text is heard twice. Teachers administering a practice test should therefore be prepared to stop the Audio CD and play the track again after each text has been heard once. Refer to the Recording Scripts for Practice Test 1 and Practice Test 2 on pages 50–52 and 54–56 to see where each text finishes. In order to answer the test questions correctly, students need to hear and fully understand certain information in the listening texts.

The listening task which follows the **Get Ready** box provides further practice for PET Listening Part 3. It is the part of the Listening test that students often find most challenging. Remind them that the words they have to write are simple words that they will know. Encourage students to write an answer, even if they're not sure; it may be correct.

Ready for PET

KEY

1 8.15/eight fifteen   2 drummer   3 weather forecast
4 wild flowers   5 *The Cookery Programme*
6 *Happy Times*

RECORDING SCRIPT

It's now five to eight and there's just time for one more song before the news, but before I do that, I'd just like to tell you about one or two things coming up later today on your local radio station.

First of all, after the eight o'clock news, at 8.15, we have our *Arts Review* programme. Debbie Clarke will be telling you about what's on in the region in the coming week, including information about theatre, cinema, and concerts. Today Debbie will also have a special guest in the studio, Kevin Jones, who is the drummer with the very successful pop band, *Splodge*. Kevin will be talking about what it's like to be the drummer rather than the lead singer in a pop band.

That's followed at 8.45 by the weather forecast. Graham Smith will be here to tell you if it's going to be wet or fine for the rest of the week. Let's hope that Graham has some good news for us. After that, at 8.50, a new series begins. Polly Brown has been out and about in the countryside this week talking to people who are interested in wild flowers. And I must say that some of those people really know a great deal about the subject.

After that, at 9.30, we have *The Cookery Programme*. James Grant will be back with some more delicious recipes, and he'll also be telling us what to look out for when we're buying fresh fruit and vegetables. And finally, at 10.15, we have this morning's radio play. *Happy Times* it's called, and it tells the story of two children's summer holiday by the seaside and something which happened that was to change their lives forever. Sounds good. So, that's it on your favourite station today. Now up to the news here is *Splodge* with their latest single, which is called '*Take me*'.

6 Writing

Encourage students to make use of the topic vocabulary in writing this story. It can be completed for homework if necessary.

10 (2) The age of communication

Topic

The topic of this lesson is communication. Aspects of this topic may come up in any part of PET. Students should be prepared to write and speak about their own experiences of various means of communication and give their views about them. They are not required to know technical vocabulary, however.

Lesson focus

The focus of this lesson is a revision of exam skills for the PET Speaking paper. Most time should be spent on this activity.

1 Speaking

As an introduction to the topic, students talk about their personal preferences when keeping in touch with people. At the same time they revise adverbs of frequency and the language of evaluation and comparison.

1   Treat this activity as fluency practice. Read through the words in the box with students first, and check that they understand them.

Divide the class into pairs, and give students any additional vocabulary that they need. Let the students take turns at giving their ideas to their partners. Encourage them to agree or disagree (politely) with each other, with reasons. Monitor and give feedback as necessary.

2   The photographs give further practice in descriptive language and the topic vocabulary. Refer students to **Unit 6 Lesson 2**, which is about describing photographs, before they begin.

Now work through the points in the **Get ready** box and refer to pages 6–7 for further information about how the Speaking test is structured and marked.

3   Students can now attempt this Part 2 Speaking task. Divide the class into pairs (or let the students choose their partners). Before they start, refer them back to the **Get ready** box in **Unit 2 Lesson 1**. Point out the standard wording of the rubric and make sure they understand the

instructions. Show them that the first sentence of the instructions is always the same, the next sentence describes the situation, and the last sentence explains what they have to do. The task usually has two elements.

Remind students that it is best to talk about *all* the pictures before making a decision; that they don't have to agree with each other; and that there is no right answer. Make sure that the students know the names of the objects in the visual. Ask them how they would describe each one if they didn't know its name. Elicit a range of paraphrases from the class.

4 Spelling is a necessary skill for Part 1 of the Speaking test. Remind students what they will be expected to do.

If possible, arrange for students to have a practice Speaking test using the material on pages 74–76 or 85–87 of the Coursebook. The Audio CD includes a recording of students doing the Speaking paper for Practice Test 1. You could go through this with students now, or once they have attempted a practice Speaking test themselves. Refer also to the **Notes on the sample Speaking test** on page 53.

2 Reading

This task extends the topic of the lesson. It practises a multiple-choice cloze task, of the type found in PET Reading Part 5. Refer students to **Unit 8 Lesson 1** for advice about this type of task.

KEY
1 B 2 C 3 A 4 D 5 B
6 B 7 A 8 B 9 D 10 C

3 Writing

The grammar transformation exercise reinforces the topic of the lesson. Remind students of the advice given in **Unit 8 Lesson 2** about this type of task, which is found in PET Writing Part 1.

KEY
1 than (using)
2 confuses/is confusing for
3 belong
4 tired
5 I would/I'd

Key to Practice Test 1

Note: all page numbers refer to the Coursebook

Paper 1 Reading and Writing

page 66 Reading PART 1
1 A 2 C 3 B 4 B 5 C

page 67 Reading PART 2
6 F 7 B 8 D 9 H 10 C

page 68 Reading PART 3
11 A 12 B 13 A 14 B 15 B 16 B
17 A 18 B 19 A 20 B

page 69 Reading PART 4
21 D 22 B 23 C 24 A 25 C

page 70 Reading PART 5
26 B 27 C 28 A 29 A 30 D 31 D
32 C 33 B 34 B 35 A

page 70 Writing PART 1
1 told / could tell
2 accurate as
3 make
4 if / when / whenever
5 on

page 71 Writing PART 2
There are 5 marks for this part. To get 5 marks the answer should include these points:

- a reason for not being able to go to the party
- an apology for not being able to go to the party
- the name of someone else who can take the photos.

More information about how this part is assessed is given on page 5.

page 71 Writing PART 3
There are 15 marks for this part.
Information about how this part is assessed is given on page 6.

Paper 2 Listening

page 72 Listening PART 1
1 B 2 B 3 C 4 C 5 C 6 B
7 A

page 73 Listening PART 2
8 A 9 B 10 C 11 A 12 C 13 B

page 73 Listening PART 3
14 England
15 374 days
16 (aero/air)planes
17 gloves
18 computer
19 brown

page 74 Listening PART 4
20 B 21 B 22 A 23 B 24 A 25 B

Key to Practice Test 2

Note: all page numbers refer to the Coursebook

Paper 1 Reading and Writing

page 77 Reading PART 1
1 A 2 C 3 C 4 B 5 A

page 78 Reading PART 2
6 B 7 E 8 H 9 A 10 C

page 79 Reading PART 3
11 A 12 A 13 B 14 B 15 B 16 A
17 B 18 A 19 A 20 B

page 80 Reading PART 4
21 C 22 A 23 D 24 D 25 B

page 81 Reading PART 5
26 B 27 D 28 A 29 D 30 C 31 C
32 A 33 B 34 B 35 C

page 81 Writing PART 1
1 from
2 have used
3 didn't / did not
4 before
5 as easy / so easy

page 82 Writing PART 2
There are 5 marks for this part. To get 5 marks the answer should include these points:

- some information introducing self
- a piece of useful information about the neighbourhood
- an offer to do something for the family

More information about how this part is assessed is given on page 5.

page 82 Writing PART 3
There are 15 marks for this part.
Information about how this part is assessed is given on page 6.

Paper 2 Listening

page 83 Listening PART 1
1 A 2 C 3 C 4 B 5 C 6 A
7 B

page 84 Listening PART 2
8 C 9 B 10 A 11 B 12 C 13 A

page 84 Listening PART 3
14 Africa
15 gold
16 shells
17 shape
18 music
19 hair

page 85 Listening PART 4
20 A 21 B 22 B 23 B 24 A 25 A

Grammar and vocabulary practice key

Unit 1

Exercise 1
1 up
2 on
3 up
4 off
5 on
6 on
7 out

Exercise 2

Across
1 sock
2 rubber
3 shower
4 ruler
5 shelf
6 towel
7 comb
8 soap

Down
1 toothbrush
2 scissors
3 watch
4 sheet
5 pencil
6 lamp
7 car
8 shampoo

Unit 2

Exercise 1
1 bookshop
2 romance
3 imagination
4 educated
5 met
6 done
7 much

Exercise 2
1 in
2 with
3 to
4 on
5 on

Unit 3

Exercise 1
1 too much
2 a lot of
3 too
4 enough
5 very

Exercise 2
pilot – aeroplane
dentist – surgery
hairdresser – salon
judge – court
lecturer – college
engineer – factory
secretary – office
sales assistant – shop
waiter – restaurant
presenter – TV station
nurse – hospital
footballer – stadium
priest – church
fisherman – ship
farmer – farm

Exercise 3
1 hairdresser
2 waiter
3 nurse
4 fisherman
5 secretary
6 presenter
7 farmer
8 footballer

Unit 4

Exercise 1
1d 9m
2g 10f
3k 11j
4i 12l
5n 13o
6b 14e
7a 15c
8h

Exercise 2
1 all rooms
2 bedroom
3 sitting room
4 bedroom/sitting room
5 all rooms
6 kitchen
7 sitting room/bedroom
8 kitchen
9 all rooms
10 kitchen
11 dining room
12 bathroom
13 bathroom
14 kitchen
15 all rooms

Exercise 3
1 impatient
2 unattractive
3 disappeared
4 Unfortunately, impossible
5 incorrectly
6 unable
7 disadvantage

Exercise 4
1 furniture
2 information
3 hair
4 spaghetti
5 coffees

Unit 5

Exercise 1

Across
1 carpark
2 map
3 lands
4 delays
5 passport
6 traffic
7 via

Down
1 check in
2 arrivals
3 rail
4 port
5 stop
6 route
7 visa
8 luggage

Exercise 2
1 by
2 on
3 on
4 out
5 off
6 in
7 up
8 slow

Unit 6

Exercise 1
1i 6g
2e 7b
3j 8f
4c 9h
5a 10d

Exercise 2
Internet: all except petrol and stamps
Supermarket: all

Exercise 3
1 dirty
2 empty
3 noisy
4 easy
5 rich
6 happy
7 boring
8 excited
9 rude
10 relaxed

Exercise 4
1 j   6 b
2 c   7 h
3 a   8 d
4 f   9 i
5 g   10 e

Exercise 5
1 any
2 some
3 any
4 some
5 any
6 any
7 some
8 some

Unit 7

Exercise 1
1 peel
2 sausage
3 pastry
4 mushroom
5 onion
6 dessert

Exercise 2
1 apologising
2 offering
3 refusing
4 regretting
5 complaining
6 promising
7 suggesting
8 agreeing
9 warning
10 disagreeing

Exercise 3
1 to eat any more
2 to boil the rice
3 her not to burn
4 her to open the
5 they were having for

Unit 8

Exercise 1
1 bird
2 tiger
3 spider
4 shark
5 rabbit
6 monkey
7 goat
8 lion

Exercise 2
1 traditional
2 wonderful
3 pleasant
4 amazing
5 surprising
6 embarrassed

Exercise 3
1 am learning
2 swim
3 go
4 work
5 reading
6 gets
7 has
8 being

Unit 9

Exercise 1

Across
1 Swimming
2 coach
3 run
4 tennis
5 bat
6 fitness
7 skis

Down
1 shorts
2 golf
3 wetsuit
4 Ice hockey
5 Rugby
6 net
7 Squash
8 prize
9 goal
10 tracksuit

Exercise 2
1c headache
2a sore throat
3b broken arm
4h high temperature
5d cut finger
6c earache
7c toothache
8e feel sick
9f twisted ankle
10g runny nose

Exercise 3
1 unless
2 If
3 unless
4 if
5 Unless
6 If

Unit 10

Exercise 1
1 exhibition
2 advertisements
3 admission
4 connection
5 director
6 communication
7 equipment
8 performance

Exercise 2
1 than
2 to
3 to
4 up
5 can't/cannot
6 from
7 get
8 such

Recording Script for Practice Test 1
Note: all page numbers refer to the Coursebook

Practice Test 1 – Paper 2 Listening

page 72 PART 1

RUBRIC = R

R   There are seven questions in this part. For each question there are three pictures and a short recording. Choose the correct picture and put a tick in the box below it.

Before we start, here is an example.

R   Where did the man leave his sunglasses?

M   Oh no! I've lost my sunglasses.
F   Well, you had them on in the car. Perhaps you left them inside?
M   No, I remember taking them off when we parked outside the restaurant. Perhaps I left them in there, or in that shop we went into, just before we had lunch.
F   No, you didn't leave them in the shop, because you put them on the table while we were eating. They must still be there. Come on. We'll go and get them.

R   The second picture is correct so there is a tick in box B.
   Look at the three pictures for question one now.

R   Now we are ready to start. Listen carefully. You will hear each recording twice.

R   One. What will the woman buy?

F   Do you need anything at the shops? I've got to go down to the chemist's because I need a new toothbrush.
M   Well, two things really – some toothpaste and some shampoo. They've both nearly run out.
F   I bought you some toothpaste yesterday. It's in a bag on the chair in the bathroom. I saw that it was nearly finished and there's enough shampoo. See you later, then.
M   Bye.

R   Two. Where is the woman's cookery book?

F   Have you seen my new cookery book?
M   I think I last saw it out in the garden on the seat under the tree.
F   Well, I was looking at it in the garden, but I've looked, and it's not there now. I brought it inside I think, but it doesn't seem to be on the dining-room table with my other things.
M   Look here it is, on the shelf with all the others. Your sister must have put it back when she came in from the garden.
F   Oh good.

R   Three. What time will the next train for Bristol leave?

M   This is an announcement for passengers travelling to Bristol this morning. Unfortunately, because of bad weather overnight, the 07.45 service to Bristol is cancelled and will not run today. The next direct train to Bristol will be the 08.25 which will depart from platform three. Those passengers for London who planned to change at Bristol should take the 08.05 service to Southampton and change there onto a London train. Tickets via Bristol will be valid on this train this morning.

R   Four. Which yoghurt does the girl choose?

M   Jill, you must be hungry. You've been studying for hours. How about something to eat?
F   Oh thanks, Dad. It is time I had a break. Have we got any of that chocolate ice cream you bought for my birthday?
M   Your brother finished it off this morning, I'm afraid. But we've got some yoghurt. Do you want that? There's banana, strawberry or lemon.
F   Oh I'm not keen on strawberry, so I'd rather have the banana. I do like the lemon but I had one earlier actually.

R   Five. Which band is the girl talking about?

M   Have you found any good music on the internet lately?
F   Yeah, I found this brilliant new band called the Black Bunnies, they've got their own website and you can download a sample track which is really cool.
M   Oh, I think I saw them on the television. Is that the band with the girl on the drums?
F   Well, there wasn't a drummer on the clip I saw, just two boys on guitar and a girl with an electric violin – one of the boys is also the lead singer.
M   Oh right.

R   Six. What did the boy get for his birthday?

F   Hey, I like the new swimming shorts! Were they a birthday present?
M   Oh thanks. Actually I bought these myself when I was at the beach last weekend.
   I asked for money for my birthday, so that I could buy myself a surfboard – but unfortunately my mum decided to get me these trainers instead.

Recording script for Practice Test 1

F	Well, they're very nice, even if they're not exactly what you wanted.
R	**Seven. Which animal will be on the television programme first?**
F	And in tonight's edition of *Animal Tales* we're going to see stories about both wild and pet animals, plus some who are not quite sure if they're wild or not. Like the parrot that escaped from its cage and lived for a week in a city park and the frog that decided to make its home in twelve-year-old Samantha James's bedroom. But before that, we're off to hear the story of Max, a six-month-old puppy who, rather like our escaped parrot, got a taste of freedom this week.
R	**That is the end of Part 1.**

page 73 PART 2

R	**Now turn to Part 2, questions 8–13.** **You will hear an interview with a woman who has written a popular novel.** **For each question, put a tick in the correct box. You now have 45 seconds to look at the questions for Part 2.** **Now we are ready to start. Listen carefully. You will hear the recording twice.**
I	Today I'm talking to the writer, Anna Zayuna. Anna, did you always want to write?
AZ	I wrote my first novel when I was thirteen. It was based on the life of a teacher. I even sent it to a publisher, but they weren't interested. When I got to college, I didn't think I could make a living as a writer. So I trained as a nurse because I wanted to help people, and forgot about writing.
I	What happened to change that?
AZ	Well, I met my husband when I was 20. I'd graduated and had my wedding within a few months of each other at the age of 22 and had the first of three children at 24, so my career was fairly interrupted. Later, when the children grew up a bit, I did a writing class as a hobby, and then got some work as a journalist as a result.
I	How were you discovered?
AZ	I wrote a short story and entered it for a competition on the internet. I won second place and my story was published in a magazine. Then I was asked to read the story on the radio. An agent heard that, and asked me to develop the story into a novel. It took me three years, and things just took off from there.
I	Is the novel about you?
AZ	I grew up in a small town which is actually the one that Sally – the little girl in the book – describes. But our families couldn't be more different. My father still runs his insurance firm and my mother's a full-time housewife. It was a lovely home life, and I definitely wasn't as brave as Sally is.
I	The book's about Sally and her horse. Do you like horses?
AZ	I've always liked them, but I'd never owned one. But when I started writing the book, I realised what a big part of the story they were going to become. It was fun visiting a stables to see how you look after them properly. It's not really the kind of work I'd like to do though.
I	What advice would you give young writers?
AZ	Oh I'd say, don't wait for the perfect time to start writing, but find some spare moments every day to do just a little. Also don't sit down and expect this beautiful stream of words to flow – you have to be patient. I had to keep going back and changing things in my book until they were right. But don't give up, because it's worth it in the end.
I	Anna. Thank you.
R	**That is the end of Part 2.**

page 73 PART 3

R	**Now turn to Part 3, questions 14–19.** **You will hear a student giving a talk about a person she admires.** **For each question, fill in the missing information in the numbered space.** **You now have 20 seconds to look at Part 3.** **Now we are ready to start. Listen carefully. You will hear the recording twice.**
F	The person I've chosen to talk about is a spaceman – whose job involves travelling in outer space. His name is Michael Foale and, although he now works mostly in the USA, he was actually born in England, and has also spent time working on the Russian Mir space-station. Michael's taken part in four space-shuttle missions and holds the US record for spending the most time

in space – that's 374 days in total – including one period of four-and-a-half months in a space-station.

As a boy, Michael was very keen on both science and flying, and chose to study physics at university. His first job after leaving university was with a company that built aeroplanes in the USA. After that, in 1987, he got a job with NASA, the US space agency, and his first space flight was in 1992.

In 1999, Michael made his first space walk and has now spent more than twenty-two hours walking in space. He is often given jobs to do during his space walks, which can be quite difficult wearing a spacesuit and gloves.

One of Michael's space walks included the most difficult thing that he has ever had to do in space. He had the job of putting a new computer in a satellite as it went around the Earth. If he'd done anything wrong, the satellite would have stopped working. The job took him 45 minutes and afterwards everything worked perfectly.

Michael says that one of the most surprising things about travelling in space is the wonderful colours you see. He says there are lots of different greens, blues and reds. And the Moon appears to be brown – which he says was the biggest surprise of all as he'd always thought of it as yellow.

Michael Foale is someone I truly admire. Thank you.

R   That is the end of Part 3.

page 74 PART 4

R   Now turn to Part 4, questions 20–25.

Look at the six sentences for this part. You will hear a conversation between a girl, Tanya, and a boy, Marek, about their holiday plans.

Decide if each sentence is correct or incorrect. If it is correct, put a tick in the box under A for YES. If it is not correct, put a tick in the box under B for NO.

You now have 20 seconds to look at the questions for Part 4.

Now we are ready to start. Listen carefully. You will hear the recording twice.

T   Hi, Marek. Are you looking forward to your holidays?

M   Oh Tanya, I can't wait!

T   Where is it you're going? Is it camping on an island somewhere or am I thinking of someone else?

M   Well, we were going camping, but my Dad's just bought a camper van, so we're going in that instead. It means you can go to other countries without having to get a flight which is good in a way, but actually I always used to enjoy sleeping in a tent.

T   Yeah, I know what you mean, but it must be nice getting to see all the scenery along the way. I have to say the flight is my least favourite part of going abroad on holiday.

M   Oh I never mind it actually – and the airport can be quite fun sometimes.

T   You must be joking! All those people and nothing to do except look round expensive shops. I mean, you always end up buying something you don't really want, just because there's nothing else to do.

M   Oh, I don't. Anyway, where are you off to this year? Florida again?

T   Well, I'm getting a bit old for Disneyland, Marek, though my little brother would still like it. We're actually going somewhere new. It's like a sports camp where you stay with lots of other kids and learn how to do different activities.

M   You mean you're going without your parents?

T   Not exactly. I mean they're there too doing whatever they want – golf in my dad's case – but you only actually see them at mealtimes.

M   Sounds cool. But will you have to look after your little brother?

T   No way. They divide you up according to age. He'll be doing football and swimming and all that, whereas I get to go water skiing.

M   Wow! Doesn't that cost a fortune?

T   Well, quite a bit so I'm just doing it on one of the days. But there's windsurfing and water polo too.

M   I see.

R   That is the end of Part 4.

You now have six minutes to check and copy your answers onto the answer sheet.

You have one more minute.

That is the end of the test.

Notes on the model Speaking test

Practice Test 1 – Paper 3 Speaking
Coursebook pages 74–76

On the course Audio CD, a sample Speaking test has been recorded. It comes between Practice Test 1 and Practice Test 2, which are both Listening tests. In the recording of the Speaking test, actors play the part of students. They perform the test tasks using PET-level language, but without mistakes of grammar, vocabulary or pronunciation.

Students should use the model Speaking test to help them understand the best way to do the tasks. Remember, the examination tests the ability to speak spontaneously and to interact with another person. This means that it is not possible to learn what to say in advance. It is, however, a good idea to practise and be ready to perform the tasks in the best way.

In the recording, each part of the Speaking test is played separately. The students are using the materials in Practice Test 1 – Speaking on pages 74–76 of the Coursebook. Students preparing for the PET Speaking test should listen to each part, think about how the students do each task, and then attempt the same tasks themselves. They should not try to remember actual words, as they will need to give their own opinions and ideas. This will, however, be easier for them once they have heard a model.

For each task, a list of things to listen for is included below. Students can either work individually, or in pairs as a classroom activity. Students may need to listen to each part more than once. They should look at the visual material on pages 75–76 of the Coursebook as they listen to Parts 2 and 3.

PART 1

In Part 1, students should answer the examiner's questions. (See page 7 of the Coursebook for more information.)

Listen and notice:

- how many questions each student is asked
- how long their answers are
- the types of questions each student is asked
- how the students make what they say interesting.

Notice also:

- when the students are asked to spell their names.

PART 2

In Part 2, students talk about the situation in a picture (see page 13 of the Coursebook for more information).

Listen and notice:

- how many times the instructions are given
- how the students begin
- how long each student speaks for
- how each student shows interest in what the other is saying
- how many of the pictures they talk about
- when they reach a decision.

PART 3

In Part 3, each student talks about a photograph (see page 40 of the Coursebook for more information).

Listen and notice:

- the topic of the photographs
- how each student begins
- the type of things they talk about
- what they do if they don't know a word.

PART 4

In Part 4, the students have a discussion on the same topic as Part 3, but giving their own opinions (see page 43 of the Coursebook for more information).

Listen and notice:

- the two things the students are asked to talk about
- how they begin
- how long each student speaks
- how each student shows interest in what the other is saying
- how they agree and disagree.

Note: the Speaking tests in Ready for PET are sample tests only. They are not actual Cambridge ESOL past papers.

Recording Script for Practice Test 2

Note: all page numbers refer to the Coursebook

Practice Test 2 – Paper 2 Listening

page 83 PART 1

RUBRIC = R

R   There are seven questions in this part. For each question there are three pictures and a short recording. Choose the correct picture and put a tick in the box below it.

Before we start, here is an example.

R   Where did the man leave his sunglasses?

M   Oh no! I've lost my sunglasses.
F   Well, you had them on in the car. Perhaps you left them inside?
M   No, I remember taking them off when we parked outside the restaurant. Perhaps I left them in there, or in that shop we went into, just before we had lunch.
F   No, you didn't leave them in the shop, because you put them on the table while we were eating. They must still be there. Come on. We'll go and get them.

R   The second picture is correct so there is a tick in box B.
Look at the three pictures for question one now.

R   Now we are ready to start. Listen carefully. You will hear each recording twice.

R   One. Where will they go on holiday?

F   We'd better start thinking about where to go on holiday this year.
If we wait too long, everything at the seaside will be booked up.
M   I'd like to do something really different this year. My boss was saying he and his wife went to stay on a farm, and they helped to look after the animals and pick the fruit. It would make a change from lying on the beach or walking in the mountains.
F   What a good idea! Let's do that. Can you ask him for the details?
M   Yes, OK.

R   Two. What are they cleaning?

F   Well, it's going to be a long job cleaning this. It's dirtier than I thought!
M   Don't worry, we've got all afternoon. Have you got two sponges and some shampoo? I'll start at the front, and you start at the back.
F   No, I want to do the wheels first. Shall we clean inside too? The seats look really dirty, and there's rubbish all over the floor.
M   Well, I told Dad that we'd wash it. If we're going to do the inside too, we need to ask for more money.
F   Good idea.

R   Three: Where is the water coming from?

M   Look, there's water all over the floor! Last time this happened you hadn't shut the fridge properly and all the ice melted.
F   Well, it's not open now. It must be that big plant in the corner. You've given it too much water as usual.
M   I haven't watered it for days, actually. And in any case, the water seems to be on the other side of it. The washing machine's been making a funny noise again lately, and the plant's next to that.
F   Yes, you're right. Look there's water all round it.

R   Four. What will they eat at the picnic?

F   What shall we take to eat at the picnic? I've got some chicken legs in the fridge.
M   Oh, not again! We always have those when we go on a picnic. Let's take the same as when we went to Scotland last year. It was delicious.
F   What, you mean the cheese sandwiches?
M   Actually, I was thinking of that pasta salad with olives and tomatoes. We could take some paper plates to eat it off. The sandwiches are what we had when we went to Wales. I don't want those again.
F   OK.

R   Five. What subject will the class do first this morning?

F   OK, now listen. There's a slight change to the timetable this morning because Marie, the French assistant, is off sick. You'll still be having computer studies and art as usual today, but it will be art instead of French after the morning break and computer studies up until the break. We hope that Serge, the other French assistant, will be able to give you your conversation class this afternoon, instead of this morning. But he's not here this morning, so we'll have to wait and see.

R   Six. Which T-shirt does the girl choose?

M   Come on Julia, hurry up and decide which T-shirt you want. I can't stand here all day!
F   Well, I like this one with lions on it, but the one with the dolphins is nice too.

Recording script for Practice Test 2

M What about this one with bears? Look, they're really cute.

F Dad I'm not wearing a T-shirt with teddy-bears on it! How old do you think I am?
OK, I'll have the dolphins, because the lions don't look very real anyway.

M Right.

R **Seven. Which suitcase does the woman buy?**

F Excuse me, I'd like to buy a suitcase, please. Can you tell me the difference between these three here?

M Well, the real leather one is the most expensive but is very good quality. The plastic one is the cheapest, but if you want my opinion, I'd buy a metal one.

F I see. That's the mid-priced one.

M It is. Everybody's using them because, although they're not the cheapest, they're almost unbreakable and quite light to carry.

F OK, I'll take it.

R **That is the end of Part 1.**

page 84 PART 2

R **Now turn to Part 2, questions 8–13.**

You will hear an interview with Stella Brady who is a professional photographer.

For each question, put a tick in the correct box. You now have 45 seconds to look at the questions for Part 2.

Now we are ready to start. Listen carefully. You will hear the recording twice.

I Stella, you're a professional photographer, when did you start?

SB Well, I entered my first photographic competition at the age of ten. I'd started taking photographs when I got my first camera at the age of eight. I didn't win that first competition, I had to wait until I was twelve for that – but I was the youngest competitor and the judge said how good I was for my age – it was great.

I So how did you learn?

SB Well, my parents bought me the camera – but they didn't know much about it. It was actually my uncle David who taught my brother and me. He took photographs for a local newspaper and when we were little, he used to take us along with him to visits by famous people, that sort of thing. My brother wasn't that interested, but for some reason I was.

I And did you go into this job straight from school?

SB No, you see, my uncle went to live in Australia when I was twelve. I missed him, but I didn't stop taking photographs and my big dream in life was to go and visit him out there. But I couldn't afford a holiday – I needed to save up some money. So I trained as an electrician and did that for two years.

I Then you went to Australia?

SB That's right. I visited my uncle, then travelled round taking photographs. I did get work with newspapers out there, but mostly I was selling photos of famous sights to tourists – that sort of thing. I realised that, although I'd learned a lot – I'd find it difficult to make a living as a photographer out there – so I came home.

I And now you've got your own photographic studio?

SB Yes, in my home town. I began with sports photography because I like football – but I soon realised that you made more money doing wedding photos. But those are not the photos I put up in my studio. I do some artistic work – photos of landscapes and things – it's more a hobby than anything else, but the studio's full of them.

I So what are your plans for the future?

SB Well, I'm thinking of developing my skills as a portrait photographer – you know – close-up photos of people that look a bit like oil paintings. It's quite hard to do actually because you want people to look natural and the light has to be right. You usually have to take hundreds of shots before you get the perfect one. But it's worth it.

R **That is the end of Part 2.**

page 84 PART 3

R **Now turn to Part 3, questions 14–19.**

You will hear a tour guide talking to some visitors in a jewellery workshop.

For each question, fill in the missing information in the numbered space.

You now have 20 seconds to look at Part 3.

Now we are ready to start. Listen carefully. You will hear the recording twice.

M Good morning. I'd like to welcome you to our jewellery workshop. Before we begin our tour, where you'll have the chance to meet some of our artists, let me tell you a little about the history of the workshop.

It was started five years ago by a group of artists from different countries who had studied here in London. Although there are also artists from Asia and South America in the group, it is artists from Africa who really lead the workshop, and the style of the pieces of jewellery made here reflects that.

You will see people making jewellery made out of many different materials. Gold is the metal that we use most of all, but you will also see both copper and silver as well. Also, don't expect to see too many expensive stones like diamonds. We do use them, but you are more likely to see shells and even sometimes seeds used instead.

When an artist makes a piece of jewellery, they usually begin with a shape, and you'll see them working from drawings as we walk around. Then they have to select a colour and a material. Many of the artists here get their ideas from music, so you'll hear some of that as we walk round too. Even so, artists often make many trial pieces before they get the design just right.

Although we do make rings, necklaces and earrings like all jewellers, this workshop is most famous for jewellery that can be worn in the hair. If you'd like to try on any of the pieces, there will be a chance to do this in the gallery and shop which we'll visit at the end of the tour.

So, if you're all ready, I'll take you …

R   That is the end of Part 3.

page 85 PART 4

R   Now turn to Part 4, questions 20–25.

Look at the six sentences for this part. You will hear a conversation between a boy, Darren, and a girl, Monica, about a football match.

Decide if each sentence is correct or incorrect. If it is correct, put a tick in the box under A for YES. If it is not correct, put a tick in the box under B for NO.

You now have 20 seconds to look at the questions for Part 4.

Now we are ready to start. Listen carefully. You will hear the recording twice.

F   I saw you at the football match, Darren. Did you have a good time?

M   Really? I didn't know you were there, Monica. Why didn't you come over and say hello?

F   Well, I saw you in the distance, but then I lost sight of you in the crowd. There were a lot of people there, weren't there?

M   Well, it was a normal sort of crowd for a home game.

F   Oh right. I have been before, but not for a couple of years. Some friends of mine are over from Italy and they wanted to see a match – so I took them.

M   And what did they think of the new stadium?

F   Well I think they're used to big stadiums like that in Italy, so they weren't that impressed – but I thought it was a great improvement on the old one.

M   Oh a lot better. I don't know whether it's worth the amount they ask for a ticket though – that's certainly gone up a lot.

F   Has it? I thought it compared quite well with the cost of any other afternoon out – you know, about the same as a concert or going to the theatre.

M   If you go every week, it mounts up though. Anyway, did you enjoy the match?

F   It was alright. But my friends reckon that football's more exciting in Italy and I think they may be right – you know, more stylish.

M   What do you mean? Our local team's very stylish and we've got two Italian players in the squad anyway.

F   I'd like to have seen a few goals though. I mean a goalless draw is not exactly what you hope to see, is it?

M   I thought the team did really well actually – they were just unfortunate not to hit the back of the net – they had plenty of chances.

F   OK, if you insist.

R   That is the end of Part 4.

You now have six minutes to check and copy your answers onto the answer sheet.

You have one more minute.

That is the end of the test.

Examples of student writing

In PET Writing Part 2, students are required to write a short communicative message, and in PET Writing Part 3 they have to write either an informal letter or a story. (For more details refer to pages 10, 37 and 38 in the Coursebook.)

A maximum of 5 marks is available in PET Writing Part 2. In this part, the focus of assessment is on successful communication of the message. Students will score high marks if they have conveyed the three points in the instructions clearly.

In PET Writing Part 3, 15 marks are available. The focus of assessment in this part is the student's ability to organize ideas clearly and to convey them using a range of language. Assessment is based on the correct use of spelling and punctuation; on accurate and appropriate use of a variety of grammatical structures; and on the use of topic-related vocabulary and linking words.

At this level, students are not expected to produce writing which is completely free from errors. A mistake that does not prevent the writer from being understood is considered less serious than a mistake that interferes with communication. Students are given credit for being ambitious in attempting a range of different structures, even if they make some errors.

The following examples were written by students attempting the Practice Tests on pages 71 and 82 in the Coursebook. The examiner's comments should be read in conjunction with the markschemes on pages 5–6 of this book. An 'adequate attempt' indicates the minimum standard neccesary to achieve a pass at PET level.

Practice Test 1, Writing Part 2

1

> Hello Sam,
> I'm really sorry, I can't come your birthday party. My mother will be operated next week so I should go there to look after her. A friend of me his name is Andy can take the photos. His mobile phone is 07777665522.
> Happy birthday!
> Nuria

Examiner's comments: 5 marks
The three points in the instructions for this task are included and expressed clearly. The minor language errors ('come your birthday party', 'My mother will be operated', 'A friend of me his name is Andy') don't prevent the message from being understood.

2

> To Sam
> Your 18th birthday party is next week. I'm sorry I can't go to the party. I am going play football match in another city and I going back too late. I'm very sorry. I think is good party.
> Martin

Examiner's comments: 3 marks
One of the points from the instructions for this task ('*suggest someone else who can take the photos*') has been left out, so this student can't score more than 3 marks. However, the other two points are expressed clearly in spite of some language errors ('*going play football*', '*I going back*', '*I think is good party*').

Practice Test 1, Writing Part 3 (letter)

3

> Dear Victoria:
> I am pleased to get your letter.
> Which school has not good and bad things? I think every one has both of them, whether is there rich people or poor people. The best of my school is having professional teachers, they are people who have given their complete life to teach and they know do it in the best way. Another good thing is because is a responsable institution, they give you all classes on time and use the appropriate material to teach easier.
> One of the bad things is my school is long way my house and so I am travelling two hours in the train every day.
> In conclusion, I say to you "Good school depend of good student."
> Please write to me again soon.
> Your friend,
> Marisa

Examiner's comment: very good attempt
This student writes confidently and is ambitious in her use of language. She produces a variety of present tenses, usually appropriately, and attempts some complex sentence patterns with '*whether*', '*who*' and '*because*'. She shows good control of school-related vocabulary ('*professional teachers*', '*responsable institution*', '*classes*', '*appropriate material*'). Ideas are clearly organized in paragraphs and some simple linking devices are used ('*Another good thing*', '*One of the bad things*', '*and so*', '*In conclusion*'). The letter begins and ends in an appropriate way. There are a few minor errors ('*whether is there*', '*they know do*

it', *'responsable'*, *'to teach easier'*, *'long way my house'*, *'depend of'*) but they are made because the student is being ambitious in her use of language and they do not prevent communication of the ideas.

4

> Dear penfriend,
> Thank you for your letter. I can tell you about my school. My school is beautiful and big, and it has a good organization. The subjects are very interesting and easy. But I have a lot to study. My school has a lot of classrooms, two shops to buy sweets and a very long stairs. In my classroom there is a TV, a video recorder, a new DVD and many computers. I love all of this in my school.
> But I hate my school when the teachers give me a lot of homework, when I can't say my ideas and when the teachers give me a surprise test.
> Bruno

Examiner's comment: adequate attempt

This student's letter has few language errors but it is very unambitious in its use of language and lacks variety. The present simple tense is the only tense used and the only complex sentence pattern attempted is with *'when'*. The student shows control of basic school-related vocabulary (*'organization'*, *'classrooms'*, *'computers'*, *'teachers'*, *'homework'*, *'surprise test'*). There is an attempt to organize the ideas into paragraphs and the linkers *'and'* and *'but'* are used. There is an appropriate beginning to the letter, and it has a signature at the end although the ending is rather abrupt.

5

> I'm lucky because my school is realy good and usualy I love it. But somtimes I just hate it. My school is in Fernando Pessoa street I go to school Monday Tusday Wedsday Thursday and Friday. I like talk my frends and play footbal. My history techer is good techer I must going the room. This all about my school.

Examiner's comment: poor attempt

It is difficult to make an assessment of this student's work as it is so short. The student has also copied the first two sentences directly from the input text. The language used is very basic, there are many errors and the meaning of the penultimate sentence is unclear. The writer makes no attempt to follow letter-writing conventions and does not address the reader directly, begin or end the letter appropriately or sign it.

Practice Test 1 – Writing Part 3 (story)

6

> The message in the sand
> Once upon a time Josh was kidnapped by some pirates. They took Josh to their boat and there an adventure started. The boy decided to escape because he was very scared. Paco, the pirate boss caught Josh and slapped him. The boy started to cry, so Paco pushed him to the sea.
> Josh was very afraid. Fortunately he saw an island and he swam towards there.
> He was very hungry and tired so he felt asleep on the sand. When he woke up he looked for a stem to fish. Later, he saw a boat coming so he wrote a message in the sand. The people on the boat never saw the message. Josh is story now.

Examiner's comment: good attempt

This student is ambitious in his use of language. He uses the past simple correctly and appropriately with a variety of regular and irregular verbs, including a passive form. He attempts some complex sentence patterns using *'because'* and *'when'*. He makes use of a good range of adventure-related vocabulary (*'kidnapped'*, *'pirates'*, *'escape'*, *'scared'*, *'caught'*, *'slapped'*, *'pushed'*). The narrative develops clearly with ideas organized in paragraphs and linked through connectors (*'Once upon a time'*, *'so'*, *'Fortunately'*, *'Later'*). Unfortunately, the meaning of the final sentence is not entirely clear, which detracts from the overall impression the story makes. There are few other language errors (*'to the sea'*, *'felt asleep'*, *'stem'*) and these do not impede understanding of the story.

7

> This is the story about three boys. They had lived a libely childhood together, during the summers they went near a sea and they had joined to play and spend their time together. Every day they went to the beach and they had used to leaves differents messages in the sand, they invented a new alphabet and they created differents signs that nobody else had untherstood. One day one of the boys was kidnaped, all the city was upset, the people went by differents places but nobody could found the boy. But the friends thought about their old play and went to the beach. There they could found the signs and they translate its to the police. A few

> hours later the police could find the house where three man had a little boy. They could rescue him without problems because they acted quickly by surprise.

Examiner's comment: adequate attempt
This student attempts to use a range of structures but there are many errors and control of past tenses is weak. There is some good use of vocabulary which is appropriate to the story ('childhood', 'spend their time', 'invented a new alphabet', 'created differents signs', 'kidnaped', 'upset', 'translate', 'rescue'). The narrative progresses smoothly through the use of time phrases ('during the summers', 'Every day', 'One day', 'A few hours later') and the connectors 'and' and 'but'. The story has a good introductory sentence and an appropriate concluding sentence. The story is not penalised for being a bit long but the extra length means there are more errors. The errors mostly do not impede understanding.

8

> One day I read the message in the sand. The message is JOHN LOVE ROSA so I am Rosa but who is John? I am walking at the beach I am looking at all peoples. Are you John? Are you John? Nobody are speaking. All people are thinking she is mad girl. I want know John. May be he is good man. Then I see my father at the beach, he have small dog. He give dog he say this dog his name is John and he is to you and I think he love you. Now I can understand the message in the sand!

Examiner's comment: inadequate attempt
This is a fairly coherent story but the language used is limited and there are many basic errors, some of which obscure the meaning. Control of verb forms is weak and there is no attempt to use anything other than present tenses. The vocabulary used is also limited. An attempt is made to use narrative markers ('One day', 'Then', 'Now') but the story is not organized into paragraphs. The story has appropriate beginning and ending sentences.

Practice Test 2, Writing Part 2

9

> Hello,
> My husband and me our flat is 34 to the left of yours. This place is so quiet but sometimes on weekend the family in the 53 like to make parties until midnight.
> Came you want with us take a delicious English tea.
> Regards, Martha and Jack

Examiner's comment: 4 marks
The three points in the instructions for this task are included and the first two points are expressed clearly in spite of some minor language errors ('My husband and me our flat', 'on weekend', 'make parties'). However, the third point, the offer, is not very clearly expressed meaning this candidate scores 4 rather than 5 points.

10

> Hello! My name is Noemi. I live here for three years. So I can give you some information about my town. There is a big supermarket at the end of this street. You can buy any kinds of food there.

Examiner's comment: 3 marks
One of the points from the instructions for this task ('offer to do something for the family') has been left out, so this student can't score more than 3 marks. However, the other two points are expressed clearly in spite of some language errors ('I live here for three years', 'any kinds of food').

Practice Test 2, Writing Part 3 (letter)

11

> Dear Daniel,
> I'm so glad to receive your letter! And I'm very happy to know you are coming in Italy!
> In my opinion, you must visit Florence, which is wonderful, and Uffizi with all the history of the Renaissance. Then you can visit Siena, Arezzo and Pisa, with the famous tower and the nature, which is wonderful.
> After enjoying yourself in this way, you can visit Assisi or Gubbio, both are beautiful as Medieval towns, and going sightseeing is like a time-travel.
> We've also got a lot of museums, good restaurants (our cousine is the best of the world) and festivals of every kind you want.
> Isn't it a fantastic reason to come?
> See you as soon as possible.
> Kisses,
> Valeria.

Examiner's comment: good attempt
This student is fairly ambitious in her use of language and attempts to employ a more than adequate range of structures, including the use of complex sentence patterns with 'which', 'After' and 'both'. She demonstrates a range of vocabulary which is more than adequate for the task ('history of the

Renaissance', 'famous tower', 'Medieval towns', 'going sightseeing', 'time-travel', 'fantastic reason'), though there is repetition of '*wonderful*'. The ideas are organized clearly in paragraphs and there is an attempt to use connecting words and phrases ('*In my opinion', 'then', 'After enjoying yourself in this way*'). The letter begins and ends appropriately and will have a positive effect on the reader. There are few errors, none of which impede communication of the ideas.

12

> My dear Rachel,
> I'm very happy you planning to visit Korea. You can find the history everywhere but I very recommend you go to Kyongju. This is beautiful place it has a lot old tumbs and casels. You like beautful montans? You can go Sorak-san national park, it very beautful place all time but in autum it very much beautful because trees are going red and gold color. Do not forget our capital city Seoul it has many intersting places for visiters. You like spicy food? You can use the chopsticks? I take you very good restaran in my city Seoul. Come to Korea soon!
> Your friend Hyung Pun

Examiner's comment: adequate attempt

This student is not ambitious in her use of language but there is an adequate range of structures. There is a fairly good range of vocabulary ('*tumbs', 'casels', 'montans', 'autum', 'capital city', 'spicy food', 'chopsticks*') but this is marred by spelling errors and repetition of some words ('*beautful', 'place*'). The ideas are organized logically but the organization would be improved by the use of paragraphs. The letter has an appropriate beginning and ending. Although there are a number of errors these do not impede communication.

Practice Test 2, Writing Part 3 (story)

13

> Emma didn't know how to find the money she needed. She wanted to buy a beautiful jacket which she had seen in a shop window. Unfortunately she had already received her pocket money and spent it on a gift. She knew that jacket it was the only one left. So she tried working like a baby-sitter, a waitress, a dog-sitter. Finally, at the end of the mounth, she had collected enought money to buy what she wanted. She run into the shop and looked at the jacket. What a terrible surprice! She realized that she had read the price wrongly. Infact it had one more zero. She felt really sad, tourned back home and ... on her bed there was a big present, and all her friends shouted "Happy Birthday". It was her birthday but she had been so concentrated in work that she hadn't remember it! The present was the jacket! What a careless and lucky girl!

Examiner's comment: good attempt

This student uses fairly ambitious language. She uses both past and past perfect tenses appropriately and mostly accurately, and attempts some complex sentence patterns with '*which*' and '*so ... that*'. There is also a range of vocabulary appropriate to the task ('*pocket money', 'spent it on', 'baby-sitter', 'waitress', 'dog-sitter', 'read the price wrongly', 'concentrated*'). The story develops well and although it is not organized in paragraphs, good use is made of linking words ('*Unfortunately', 'So', 'finally', 'Infact*'). The story comes to an effective resolution and the errors do not impede communication.

14

> Emma didn't know how to find the money she needed. She thinks in diferents forms to collect money. One of the ideas are collect money selling lemonade. Other way for collect money was working in a fast food restaurant six hours a day but she only have one mounth to collect $130 and working in the restaurant she will collect $120. She goes to her best friend house Sue to talk with her. They talk and talk and then Sue say this: Why don't you work in the fast-food restaurant and when you finish working you come to sell lemonade. Emma liked the idea of doing that and she starting do it. At the end of the mounth she collect $150 and Emma could buy the bike she want.

Examiner's comment: adequate attempt

This student's use of language is fairly unambitious. The initial sentence (provided) is in the past tense but there are few past tenses in the rest of the story. Complex sentence patterns are rarely attempted and ideas are mainly connected using '*and*' and '*but*'. There is an adequate range of vocabulary for the task ('*selling lemonade', 'fast food restaurant*') although there is repetition of '*collect*'. The story develops well through the use of appropriate linkers ('*One of the ideas', 'Other way', 'then', 'At the end of the mounth*') although ideas are not organised into paragraphs. The story comes to a successful resolution and the errors do not impede communication.

Wordlist

Unit 1 Lesson 1
advice
block capitals
to collect
to complete (a form)
computer games
(to go) dancing
date of birth
details
driving
to enjoy
to explain
free time
hill walking
(to go) horse riding
instruction
to be interested (in s.thing)
interesting
Internet
keep-fit exercises
notice
occupation
package
personal
shop assistant
to sign (your name)
signature
to spell
to study
suggestion
to surf (the Internet)
surname
warning
watersports
windsurfing

Unit 1 Lesson 2
to accept
to agree
armchair
to attend
books
to brush
to check
climate
to comb
daily
to describe
desk
to dial
dishes
to dust
to feed
to forget
furniture
(a pair of) glasses
hair
to hand in
to imagine
international
interview
to invent
invention
to iron
to join in
make-up
medicine
meeting
message
mirror
to miss
mobile phone
to offer
palace
parcel
pet
philosopher
(what a) pity
to plug in
popular
to put away
to put on
to put up

radio
scientist
shirt
shoelaces
(a pair of) shoes
situation
soap
(a pair of) socks
to suggest
to take off
teeth
to thank
to tidy
to tie
to turn on
to turn up
umbrella
walkman
(to do the) washing-up
worried

Unit 2 Lesson 1
blackboard
boring
cakes
CD (compact disc)
to cook
correct
the cost (of s.thing)
document
(to send an) e-mail
enjoyable
equipment
favourite
to fry (an egg)
fun
to be good (at s.thing)
hobby
incorrect
ingredients
keyboard
to last
length
to look forward (to s.thing)
magazines
mouse
newspaper
to respond
screen
stuff
textbook
useful
video cassette
video player
videotape

Unit 2 Lesson 2
adult
adventure story
to advertise
amusing
autobiography
to belong (to s.body)
biography
bookshop
to borrow
to take care
charming
to create
cruel
damage
danger
daughter
deadly
delighted
design
dinosaur
to disappear
discover
distant
to encourage
enemy
excitement

exciting
film star
gossip
grandson
to guide
to happen
heavy
hero
horror
humour
to hunt (for s.thing)
(a police) inspector
to investigate
to invite
journey
kind
to lend
to look for
to manage (to do s.thing)
marvellous
murder
mystery
old-fashioned
opinion
to pass (time)
planet
powerful
to prepare
to prove
to publish
realistic
to recognize
to request
to respect
romance
science fiction
secret
shadow
to shoot
spaceship
space travel
a spoonful (of s.thing)
stage
to steal
stormy
strange
successful
suitable
surprise
teenager
thriller
universe
victim
visitor
to win
wise

Unit 3 Lesson 1
accommodation
answerphone
arrangements
available
belongings
binoculars
booking
brochure
(to go) camping
campsite
credit card
destination
to discuss
downstairs
employee
excursion
experience
expert
facilities
first-aid kit
guest house
guidebook
handicrafts
hotel
luggage

map
market
minimum
mosquito net
nervous
nightlife
official
to pack
package holiday
passenger
photographs
(to have a) picnic
postcards
preparation
to prevent
to provide (s.thing for s.body)
to put up
(to make a) reservation
to run out (of s.thing)
scenery
shells
shower
sightseeing
souvenirs
(to go) sunbathing
(a pair of) sunglasses
suntan lotion
to supply
to take turns
tinned food
tour
training course
travel agency
trip
truck
unattended
value
variety
vegetables
vehicle
wallet
wildlife

Unit 3 Lesson 2
to accompany
advertisement
appearance
application form
to apply (for a job)
architect
artist
bank clerk
biologist
businessman/woman
chemist
choice
to decide
decision
doctor
to earn (a salary)
to employ
employment
engineer
to fill in (a form)
fortunately
to get up
to govern
government
hard work
insurance
journalist
lawyer
lift
lucky
manager
microscope
musician
to organize
physicist
to pick (s.one) up
police officer
profession
qualification

recording studio
responsible
to retire
retirement
rules
satisfactory
staff
stressful
strike
to succeed
success
traffic
typical
unfamiliar
uniform
unsuitable
unusual
vegetarian
worried

Unit 4 Lesson 1
balcony
basement
bath
bathroom
bedroom
bedside table
blanket
blinds
block of flats
calculator
chest of drawers
coffee table
cooker
curtains
cushions
dining room
dishwasher
dressing table
fridge
garage
garden
hairdryer
hallway
kitchen
lamp
living room
mirror
packed lunch
pillows
to remember
seaside
shampoo
sheet
sink
sofa
stairs
storeroom
towel (rail)
wardrobe
washbasin
waterproof
wood

Unit 4 Lesson 2
to advise
amount
amusing
anxious
attitude
attractive
bald
blond(e)
bored
boring
careful
careless
celebration
cheerful
to compare
to complain
confident
to correspond

curly
to develop
development
dull
education
fair
foolish
funny
hard-working
high school
honest
intelligence
lazy
to measure
middle-aged
miserable
pretty
professor
psychologist
to recommend
serious
shy
slim
smart
to smile
speed
strong
truthful
ugly
understanding
university
weak

Unit 5 Lesson 1
admission
to arrange
attraction
breakage
ceiling
changing rooms
to climb
collection
department store
discount
display
entrance (fee)
to exhibit
giftshop
gift-wrapping
to hire
home-made
in advance
to inform
items
leaflet
picture gallery
pleasant
plenty
public
reasonable
to receive
refreshments
representative
to reserve
ruin
sports centre
surrounding
to touch
traditional
view
weigh
well-known

Unit 5 Lesson 2
appointment
arrival
attendant
bank account
boarding pass
carriage
to catch
to check in
to check out (of)
convenient

to cross out
to disturb
to draw out
driver
explanation
to fill in (a form)
forename
furnished
gate
to get in
to get off
to get on
to give in
to hurry up
instead of
to land
to lend
license
luggage
meter
passenger
personal
pilot
platform
position
report
station
stop
to switch on
to take off
ticket
timetable
to turn over
underground

Unit 6 Lesson 1
acceptance
bargain
belt
boot
buttons
charge
cheque
clothing
collar
cotton
department
electrical
escalator
example
fashion
fashionable
goods
invitation
lift
out of order
parachute
pocket
reason
receipt
receive
reduce
refusal
repair
sale
shopping centre
silk
skirt
sleeve
speciality
to spend
spices
spots
stall
street market
stripes
sweater
tie
(a pair of) tights
tip
to try on
topic
upstairs
vegetables
wool
zip

Unit 6 Lesson 2
advantage
convenient
crowded
dangerous
dirty
employment
entertainment
forest
fresh air
inconvenient
lonely
noisy
objects
peaceful
polluted
relaxing
rice
safe
spoon
stressful
sunny
traffic
transport
vehicle
way (of life)

Unit 7 Lesson 1
to add
bananas
beans
beef
burgers
butter
carrots
cheese
chicken
duck
fork
garlic
grapes
hard-boiled egg
herbs
impressive
knife
lamb
mayonnaise
to mix (together)
mixing bowl
mixture
mushrooms
olives
onions
oranges
owl
peas
pepper
plums
potato
to pour
recipe
salt
sausages
seeds
selection
sharp
snack
a spoonful (of s.thing)
steak
tasty
tomatoes
tomato sauce
triangle
tuna fish

Unit 7 Lesson 2
to afford
to allow
to annoy
argument
average
to blame
circumstances
cupboard
divide
dizzy

early
to expect
fancy
to find
to fit
fussy
knock
to lead to
likely
lucky
to mind
miserable
to operate
opinion
privacy
regret
relationship
to repair
to review
selfish
to separate
to share
shelf
storage
tidiness
to tidy up
wardrobe

Unit 8 Lesson 1
to appear
to attack
bat
to be born
bear
bee
to breathe
brilliant
to bury
changeable
cheerful
chicken
clear
clouds
coal
coast
cool
countryside
cow
damp
to defend
depressed
to destroy
to dig up
disease
dolphin
to dry up
dull
dusty
elephant
encouraging
environment
extraordinary
extremely
eyesight
to fall down
fields
to fight
fine
to fly
foggy
forecast
freezing
frost
giraffe
gold
goldfish
gorilla
height
horse
human
hunger
inhabitants
iron
jump
kick
kitten
lightning

minerals
mist
monkey
mouse
nature
to overtake
owner
pavement
pet
to pick
pigeon
to pollute
to pour
poverty
to prevent
rabbit
rain
to reach
to realize
to rescue
rubbish
to set out
shark
shower
to slip
snake
snow
spider
to spoil
storms
to strike
to suffer
sunshine
to tear
thunder
tiger
tongue
urgent
warm
to watch
weather
to weigh
wind

Unit 8 Lesson 2
to admire
beach
border
to break (down)
bush
camel
canal
canoe
cave
cliff
climb
continent
to cross
desert
director
distance
district
eagle
edge
to float
to flood
foreign
frontier
to hang
hole
interval
irrigation
island
jungle
local
location
mountain
mud
nest
on foot
on horseback
passport
path
project
to promise
to provide
restful

rock
row
ruins
sand
scenery
to set (the video)
shade
to shine
shore
to smell
soil
speed
stream
temperature
to tour
track
villain
waterfall
wave
website

Unit 9 Lesson 1
adventurer
to attend
balloon
baseball
to brush
circus
clown
crab
to discover
driving test
entertainment
envelope
facts
to fail
to feed
flower
frightened
golf
ground
gymnastics
hammer
handle
hockey
to introduce
to invent
judo
juggling
nails
needle
net
notepaper
paint
pins
poetry
pot
to present
racket
refreshing
safety (rules)
sailing
scissors
seeds
skiing
skill
to slide
spade
stamp
table tennis
to take up
training
tunnel
watering can
windsurfing
workshop

Unit 9 Lesson 2
accident
to ache
ambulance
aspirin
benefit
blood
to consider
to cure
deaf

deep
dentist
disease
documentary
to fall over
flu
Get well!
grateful
healthy
hearing (aid)
hospital
hurt
jogging
lifestyle
to look (after)
opppportunity
patient
sickness
sore throat
stress
to take care (of)
toothache
unhealthy
valuable

Unit 10 Lesson 1
action (film)
actor
audience
backing (group)
camera
channel
characters
chat room
to clap
clubbing
to come up
comedian
commercial
crew
curtain
dancer
delicious
director
disc jockey
drummer
film critic
interval
interviewer
lead (singer)
lines
performance
pianist
play
plot
pop group
to practise
presenter
programme
region
reviews
screen
series
singer
soap opera
(to be) sold out
stage
studio
violinist
wet

Unit 10 Lesson 2
communication
confused
to contact
face-to-face
fax
letters
misunderstanding
to pay attention
to phone
recent
relaxed
respect (for)
screen
skills
word-processing